GRAYWOLF FORUM 3

The Business of Memory

GRAYWOLF FORUM 3

The Business of Memory

The Art of Remembering in an Age of Forgetting

Edited by
CHARLES BAXTER

GRAYWOLF PRESS : SAINT PAUL

Publication of this volume is made possible in part by a grant provided by the Minnesota State Arts Board through an appropriation by the Minnesota State Legislature, and by a grant from the National Endowment for the Arts. Significant support has also been provided by Dayton's, Mervyn's, and Target stores through the Dayton Hudson Foundation, the Bush Foundation, the McKnight Foundation, the General Mills Foundation, the St. Paul Companies, and other generous contributions from foundations, corporations, and individuals. To these organizations and individuals we offer our heartfelt thanks.

Additional support for this publication was provided by the Patrick and Aimee Butler Family Foundation and the Star Tribune.

"DON'T STOP" (Christine McVie)
© 1976, 1977 Fleetwood Mac Music (BMI)
All Rights Reserved—Reprinted by Permission

Lydia Davis's essay, "'Remembering the Van Wageners,'" first appeared in *The Southern Humanities Review,* Spring 1999.

Steve Erickson's essay, "American Nomad," was published in *American Nomad,* Henry Holt and Company, New York, 1997, and is reprinted here with some slight changes. Best efforts have been made to gain permission from the publisher.

Margot Livesey's essay, "The Third Servant," first appeared in *Five Points,* Fall 1998.

In James A. McPherson's essay, "'El Camino Real,'" excerpts are quoted from *The Kiss* by Kathryn Harrison, published by Random House, Inc. Copyright © 1997 by Kathryn Harrison. Reprinted by permission of Random House, Inc.

Published by
Graywolf Press
2402 University Avenue, Suite 203
Saint Paul, Minnesota 55114
All rights reserved.

www.graywolfpress.org

Published in the United States of America.

ISBN 1-55597-287-X
ISSN 1088–3347

2 4 6 8 9 7 5 3 1
First Graywolf Printing, 1999

Library of Congress Catalog Card Number: 98-88485

Cover photograph: Debra Raven, Photonica
Series and cover design: A N D

Contents

Introduction

.   .   .   .

In a review of a recently published book of memoirs, Frank Conroy somewhat irritably notes: "Memoirs to the left of us. Memoirs to the right of us. A blizzard of memoirs good, bad and indifferent." The first implicit metaphor, of memoirs as cannons aimed at the Light Brigade of readers, and the second one, of memoirs as stinging snowflakes in a blinding storm, leave little doubt about Conroy's worries concerning the genre. But it's still a puzzling triad of sentences. What *good* precipitation could Mr. Conroy possibly have in mind when he uses that adjective and attaches it to the blizzard? Still, he himself has written a grand memoir, *Stop-Time*, and has therefore contributed to the blizzard in question. Like the rest of us, he too has trafficked in the business of memory.

Cannons, blizzards. *Mud slides* of memoirs. Readers and critics these days have had strong opinions about the writing of memoirs, and they have not been slow to express them. Feelings run high on this subject, and there has been considerable name-calling in the critical literature. In fact, the metaphors that Frank Conroy has chosen are mild compared to some that have been deployed. Thanks to the work of Christopher Lasch, the word *narcissism*, for example, appears ubiquitously in discussions of contemporary memoirs. Memoirs by Kathryn Harrison, Frank McCourt, Tobias Wolff, and some of the contributors to the volume you hold in your hand, have created a considerable stir; they have managed to get people excited and upset.

All these attacks upon the memoir boom probably screen a larger issue having to do with the role of memory, both personal and impersonal, in an information age. Memory and subjectivity are inevitably joined here. They have to be. And subjectivity, in many of its forms, is now being contested. You may possess subjectivity, you may even be a subject yourself, but it is sometimes considered to be in bad and somewhat narcissistic taste to say so. Subjectivity leads to self-indulgence and finally to narcissism.

Communities are sacrificed for the sake of the self. The public realm dies as everyone turns inward.

Still, not every expression of subjectivity (which has to be understood by means of memory) can be a side effect of narcissism. Furthermore, the business of memory is not just the business of memoir writers. It is also Bill Gates's business. Anyone involved with artificial intelligence and electronic data processing has been touched by it. Memory, to put it another way, has become a profitable if somewhat controversial growth industry. You can now buy more memory at your corner computer store, but only your computer can have it.

You *can* buy memory enhancers at the vitamin store for yourself—today in a stack of junk mail I received an advertisement that warns, "SENILITY EPIDEMIC—1 in 5 over 60 Affected!"—but the remedies are expensive and unproven scientifically. The remedy is not as significant, I'm certain, as the fear-of-forgetting that this brochure addresses.

The storage and retrieval of impersonal data and the remembering and forgetting of personal experiences have become linked somehow. And they are both causing excitement and anxiety in the culture at large. The real questions might be phrased in the following way: What is remembered? And why? And how? And why, in the professional-managerial class, has memory become such an obsession?

I see that I am being a bit circuitous. Let me start again. The first volume in the new Graywolf Forum Series, *Tolstoy's Dictaphone: Technology and the Muse* (edited by Sven Birkerts), published in 1996, dealt with the fate of the book in an electronic age. This third volume in the Graywolf Forum Series might be considered an adjunct to the first. When I first came up with this topic, my intention had been to gather together essays having to do with the fate of personal memory in an age of information-glut. In a culture afflicted with data-nausea, I thought, everyone begins to hoard and value the autobiographical, a refuge safe from irony. I had suspected that computers have altered the way in which we think about our own memories and that artificial memory had in effect raised the value of personal memory to unprecedented levels. I was also curious about the marketing of personal memory, its commodification on the literary market. What a curious experience it must be, I thought, for any writer when his or her memoirs go on sale and the private life has been converted into a public and commercialized event.

. . . .

I proposed this topic to several writers whose work I admired, and they agreed to write on the subject.

But what actually happened, as the essays gradually arrived on my doorstep, was that the topic under discussion had altered. The question of subjectivity is answered in these essays by several usable definitions of what is private and what isn't. Narcissism as a topic enters this discussion because narcissism can be understood as an overspillage of what should be private into the public sphere. The business of memory helplessly becomes a matter of the private and the public from the moment that any memory is committed to paper. At the same time that we're worried about our memories, we're worried about privacy. Memoirs have a way of focusing both those anxieties.

Perhaps there really isn't any privacy anymore. I am writing this introduction the day after Kenneth Starr's report on President Bill Clinton was delivered to Congress. This same week, Joyce Maynard's book containing her account of her relationship—it was not exactly an affair—with J. D. Salinger has been reviewed widely. Salinger is now famous for two considerable accomplishments: his writing, and his privacy. He is, it might be said, the most private public (that is to say: famous) man in America. To a certain degree, he has been stripped of his privacy by Joyce Maynard, just as Bill Clinton was stripped of his by the combined efforts of Linda Tripp, Ken Starr, and, finally, Monica Lewinsky. As we all know, our credit histories and records of our purchases are stored in mainframes, somewhere. Much is known about every one of us, although not what we would probably like to have known.

Most of the essays in this volume study the effect of memory's peculiar privacy. Some of the authors included here do their best to chart the effect of turning a private memory into a public event and the betrayal (self-betrayal or betrayal of others) that that action sometimes requires. And others deal with the *art* that that action always requires.

This is of particular interest because all of the contributors to this book are *literary* writers. I say this proudly on their behalf and without apology. They are all practitioners of poetry or fiction or both. Their particular interest in memory and the effect of turning something private into a public event is filtered through literary—rather than purely scientific, psychoanalytic, sociological, or commercial—sensibilities. That is why, I think, so many of the writers here are anxious and eloquent about privacy's relationship to memory, and the way in which what has once been loved and seen and experienced can be turned into words.

. . . .

What I hadn't anticipated was that the dialectical opposite of memory, its shadow and demon, *forgetting*, would move to the center of so many of these essays. Forgetting is, it seems, often more fascinating than remembering. We can, after all, name our memories and locate them when we engage in negotiations with our past and our histories. This is the historic territory of the autobiography from the Italian Renaissance onward. Our recollections are our familiars, both the good and the bad, even when we write them down and put them into a book. But forgetting as an act and a state of mind is harder to name, and its story is harder to tell. It is a haunted subject. Everything forgotten becomes ghostlike. To put it cryptically, we are never familiar with what we have forgotten. We are always alienated from it. What is forgotten is unnamable until the moment it becomes memory again, if it ever does. The forgotten resists narrative and confounds it. We don't even have a name for the antimemoir, though *oubliette* comes close. "I am writing an oubliette. Its pages are blank." Oscar Levant comes to mind: *Memoirs of an Amnesiac*.

By contrast to the beauties and terrors of memory, forgetting tells almost no story at all. Almost. It is that "almost" that so many of the writers here have tried to approach, describe, and name.

The majority of these essays approach memory, it seems, through the back door. What we talk about when we talk about memory is—often—what we have forgotten and what has been lost. The passion and torment and significance seem to lie in that direction. We are now the children of Beckett more than the children of Proust. As dark as this prospect might seem, the contributors to this volume have made it an occasion for passionate writing, exuberant celebration, even high and low comedy. The range of voices here is enormous and is matched by the subject matter. These essays stick to the business at hand, and they are, well, *unforgettable*.

CHARLES BAXTER
October 1998

we are familiar with what we remember
what we have forgotten is strange
(we are strangers to what we
have forgotten) — "hamlet"

GRAYWOLF FORUM 3

The Business of Memory

So Long Ago

.   .   .   .

by
RICHARD BAUSCH

see 9 Indulge me, a moment.

I have often said glibly that the thing which separates the young from
the old is the knowledge of what Time really is; not just how fast, but how
illusive and arbitrary and mutable it is. When you are twenty, the idea of
twenty years is only barely conceivable, and since that amount of time
makes up one's whole life, it seems an enormous thing—a vast, roomy expanse, going on into indefiniteness. One arrives at forty with a sense of the
error in this way of seeing, and maturity, um, can be said to have set in.

And the truest element of this aspect of the way we experience time, of
course, is the sense of the nearness of time past.

I have a memory of being bathed by my father on my seventh birthday.
Morning, rainy light at a window. The swish and wash of lukewarm
water. My own body, soft-feeling and small under the solid strong hands,
lathered with soap. I said, "Well, I guess I'm a big boy now."

He said, "No, not quite."

I remember feeling a bit surprised, perhaps even downcast, that he
didn't simply agree with me, as most of the adults in our large family usually did. He ran the towel over me, ruffled my hair with it, drying me off.
I went across the hall into my room, and dressed for the April day. Base-
ball season was starting.

Let me go back there for a little while, to that bath, my seventh birthday. At the time, I wasn't old enough to understand the difference between
the humoring of children, which is a large part of any talk with them, and
truth telling, which is what my father did. I loved his rough hands on me,

3

and the smell of him—aftershave, and cigarettes, and sometimes the redolence of my mother's Chanel.

He hated lies, and lying. He was a storyteller, and he must have learned early how to exaggerate and heighten things, to make the telling go better, to entertain and enthrall. He was so good at it. He could spin it out and do all the voices and set the scene and take you to the laughs, and there simply *had* to have been elements that he fabricated. And yet he hated lies. Any trouble you ever got into in our house always had to do with that: you learned very early that even if you *had* done something wrong, something for which you wanted some kind of an excuse, or explanation, it had better not involve telling a lie.

I was often in some kind of mischief at school—my twin, Robert, and I had a talent for making other kids laugh, and for imitating our teachers' gestures and voice mannerisms. Well, we were the sons of a storyteller. Neither of us liked school very much; and the teachers, the nuns of Saint Bernadette's, knew it. They kept tabs on us. They were at some pains to discipline us. And whenever we got into a scrape at school, we lived in dread that our father would ask us, that evening, how things had gone at school. I remember sitting at the dinner table as he and my mother told stories, or commented happily on the various people—friends and family—who inhabited our lives then. Bobby and I would sit there in awful anticipation of the question: "How was school today?" You couldn't gloss over anything—you couldn't use a cover-all word like *fine*. You had to be specific, and you had to tell it all, the truth. You were *compelled* to do so by what you knew of the value he set upon the truth. And never mind philosophical truth, or the truth of experience, really; he wanted to know what happened in the day, what was said and done, and how it went—*that* kind of truth.

I have no memory—not even a glimmer—of how and when we learned that this was what he expected from us, and that the surest way to earn his displeasure was by lying to him. I don't have much of a memory of him telling us this; I recall him talking about how it was a thing *his* father expected, but by then I was in my teens, and I understood it then as an echo of a kind, a source.

All right.

I remember being surprised that in my father's truthful opinion I was not a big boy yet. I remember that we had two boys our age living next door to us, and that this took place on Kenross Avenue in Montgomery County, Maryland. I know intellectually that the year was 1952, and that Truman was still president. I could not have said who Truman was then,

. . . .

and I recall that a few months later, in the summer, when the Republican Convention was on our little General Electric black-and-white television, I saw all those people in the arena, with Eisenhower standing there on the podium, and I guessed the number to be everyone in the world. "No," my father said, "It's not even a small fraction of the number." I didn't know the word *fraction* and yet I understood what he meant.

Sometime around then I saw film of the war that had just ended, and I was told by my mother that another war was going on, in Korea. A summer evening—we were driving past an army post, and I had seen the anti-aircraft guns, the olive drab barrels aimed at the sky. I wondered aloud why we couldn't hear the guns.

"It's on the other side of the world, honey. Thousands of miles away."

In 1952, my mother was thirty-four years old. Now, I'm almost twenty years older than that, and this is the math I'm always doing—have been doing, like a kind of mental nerve-tic, since I was twenty-seven years old, and a father for the first time myself.

When my son Wes was fourteen months old, we moved to Iowa, where I attended the Writers' Workshop. I spent a lot of time with him that year, and as he grew slightly older I decided to conduct a sort of experiment: I'd see if I could manage to keep in his memory the times we had at Iowa—the swing set and sandbox outside the Hawkeye Court Apartments, the little amusement park by the river in Iowa City, with its Ferris wheel and its kiddie train. I'd ask him about it, almost daily: "Do you remember the swing set? The sandbox? Do you remember how I used to push you on the swings, and you didn't want to go in the house? Remember the summer nights when it would be getting dark, and we'd go to that park and ride in the kiddie train?" Yes, he remembered. He was three, and then four, and then five, and he remembered. He offered elements of that time, so he wasn't merely remembering *my* memory: yes, the swing set and the sandbox—but did I remember the red wagon that got stuck there, and then buried there by the other children? I did. Yes, the kiddie train, but remember the buffalo? Yes, there had been a small enclosure with Bison standing in it; the big Ferris wheel, yes, but did I remember riding it and being stopped at the very top?

Oh, yes.

I had begun to think I might be able to help my son carry that part of his life with him into his own adulthood—earliest memories that have chronological shape. It became important that he have it all to keep. And then one winter evening, as we were riding in the car on the way to a movie, I asked him about Iowa again, and he recalled nothing—it was all simply gone. I asked him about the swing set, the sandbox, the park, the train, the Ferris wheel, even the buffalo. To each one he said, "No." Innocently, simply, without the slightest trace of perplexity or anything of what I was feeling, which was sorrow. You could see him striving to get something of it back, but it was like a game, and there was nothing. No, he had no recollection of any of it. I don't think it had been more than a week or two since we had gone through this little litany of memory, and even so it had all disappeared from his mind, and my description of it was only a story, now.

■ ■ ■

When I was fifteen, my great-grandmother, Minnie Roddy, died. Minnie had for the most part raised my mother, because Minnie's daughter had had to go to work for the government when my mother was still a baby. They all lived with my aunt Daisy, Minnie's sister, in a big sprawling Victorian house with a wide porch that had blue-gray painted boards and white trim. When Minnie began to fail, my mother went over there, and we later learned, through the talk of the adults in the rooms of the two houses, that she was holding the old woman in her arms in the last moments. Minnie used to tell me stories, sitting in the breakfast nook, by the windows where younger children ran. Summer evenings, the cousins and aunts and uncles out on the lawn, throwing horseshoes. The bell-like clang of the metal on metal when someone hit one of the posts, or scored a ringer or a leaner. Fireflies rising in the shallow pools of shade in the spaces between the houses, in the cloud-shaped willow tree—you couldn't see its trunk for the drooping filamental mass of its branches—at the edge of the property. Minnie talking, telling me about coming from Ireland on a ship; about her husband—who had come to America after killing a man in a fight one afternoon in a pub in Dublin. Her voice would trail off, and the louder voices out the window would distract me. I'd nod and pretend to listen. I was always reading books, as Bobbie was, but it showed more on me, and I was the one, after all, who believed that I had a vocation. I was planning for the priesthood. Minnie Roddy would say, "You'll grow up and tell these stories. You'll grow up and be a writer."

And she would go on talking, unscrolling her memory of earlier days, of my mother as a young girl; of Ireland, and a childhood spent, for the most part, in the latter part of the nineteenth century. I didn't hear most of it. I nodded and pretended to listen, while this woman—this tiny slip of a lady with her wire-framed glasses and her clear large blue eyes—tried to give me treasure, something to store up, for the arrival of a season I was not and am not ready for.

When she died, it was decided that Bobby and I were old enough to attend the funeral. I felt a strange detached curiosity about the whole thing: I was actually going to see a dead person. I told one of the other boys in my class, speaking it out with a sort of quiet, fake-brave shrug. "I'm going to see a dead person today."

"Who?"

"My great-grandmother."

"Jesus, no kidding?"

I was, I suppose, even a little proud of the fact. Minnie had lived to great age, and her going seemed natural enough, and so far away from my own life and world that I could only think of it in a sort of abstract haze. I was still young enough and egocentric enough to be unable quite to imagine my own demise.

The day of the funeral was bright and chilly. I don't recall whether it was spring or fall. It wasn't summer, because I was in school. I think it was fall. We rode with our parents to the funeral home, and I was like a secret traveler in the backseat, planning my exploration of this curiosity, death, this unreal element of the life I was in so permanently. I was wildly curious; I understood, according to the tenets of the faith I had been raised in that Minnie Roddy would not be there, but only her body, the empty vessel she had vacated. She was in that blue elsewhere that I associated with the sky, and we could now pray to her.

Blue is the important color, here.

Standing over the box where she lay, looking like a bad likeness of herself, I saw the forking, colorless veins in her bony hands, the fingers of which were wound with a black rosary; and I saw the blue place at her earlobe, where blue did not belong. I marked it, and knew that I would never forget it.

This sounds as though I were marking things with the flaccid, nervous sensitivity of one of those pretentious people who like to think of themselves as a romantic central figure in their own drama: the incipient artist, observing everything with the intention of later recording it. I do not mean it this way at all, and it was not like that at all. I was a child, still. I knew next to nothing about anything, especially about myself. And I don't know that I have learned much since then, either.

I suppose I have to admit that it might just be impossible to have it both ways: to claim that I was not that hypersensitive romantic figure, the artist-as-a-young-man, and still report the impressions of a moment like that one, standing over the body of a woman who had lived a life so separate from mine, and nothing like mine, and whose reality could not have anticipated that she would be a figure in my speech, a character in a story I would tell, even as she told me about all the living she had seen and done, and I pretended to listen. In any case, I do not mean this the way it will sound. I mean to express the quality of a memory, in order to say something about this life we live, so much of which is fugitive, so much of which is lost in the living of it.

The room we were in was banked with flowers, and there were chairs in rows, as though someone might give a lecture, or a homily. Minnie's coffin looked to have been where it was long enough for this prodigious wall of flowers to grow up on three sides of it. There was a dim light, a candle burning at one end. The light was brightest where she lay, with her eyes shut in a way that made you understand they would not open again. The skin looked oddly transparent, like the synthetic skin of a doll. And there was the blue place at the ear, the place, I knew, where the cosmetics of the mortician hadn't quite taken. I stood there and looked with a kind of detached, though respectful silence at this, aware of it not as death, quite, but death's signature. I was conscious of the difference. I spent my minute there, head bowed, and then walked back to my seat at the rear of the room, with the other young people, all in their early teens, like me. I saw my mother and my aunt Florence come from where I had just been, and my mother had a handkerchief that she held to her nose. She sobbed, once. Earlier, when we had arrived, Florence had come up to my mother and said, "You scared the bejesus out of me." I don't know—or I don't remember—what this was about; I think it had something to do with what had gone on last night, at the viewing. Perhaps my mother had gotten woozy, or swooned. It was the first time I had ever heard the word *bejesus*.

Florence and my mother sat down, and a priest led us in the rosary. If he said anything about the woman who lay behind him in the long box, I don't recall it. We were in the room for a time, and then people began to file out. I remained in my seat, and I have no idea why. Others crossed in front of me, and maybe I was saying my own prayers—it seems to me now that I must have felt some pang of guilt for my oddly remote observation of everything, and was trying to say the words of a prayer, repeating them inwardly in an attempt to say them not out of automatic memory but actually to enter into the meaning of them:

> Hail Mary, full of grace, the Lord is with thee. Blessed art thou among women and blessed is the fruit of thy womb, Jesus. Holy Mary, Mother of God, pray for us sinners, now and at the hour of our death, Amen.

The others were all filing quietly out of the long room, and I saw the mortician step to the side of the casket, where we had each stood only moments before. With a practical sureness, the nearly offhand familiarity of experience, he reached into the white satin that ringed Minnie Roddy's head, and pushed downward on it, a tucking motion, and Minnie slipped from her sleeping pose. Her head dropped down into that box like a stone.

Something must have shown in my face; and the mortician's wife—let us call them the Hallorans, because I no longer recall the name—saw the change in my features. Later, as I was getting into the back of my father's car, Aunt Florence leaned in and said, "Honey, Mrs. Halloran wanted me to tell you that Mr. Halloran was only making it so Minnie could rest better."

I nodded. I don't believe I said anything. It was almost as if I had stumbled upon someone in a privy act; I felt the same kind of embarrassment. But there was something else in it, too, a kind of species-thrill: this was the human end, a reality I was not expecting. I am trying to express this as exactly as I can, and it is finally inexpressible. I know that all my fascination was gone, and I sat there in the back of the car, looking out at the sunny streets of Washington, D.C., and felt numb, far down.

That memory is as present to me as the moment, almost a decade earlier, when I said to my father that I was a big boy, and he told me the truth, that I was not a big boy. Not yet. And those memories are as near as the memory of asking, in the first line of this story, for your indulgence.

Of course, this is not an original perception; yet one arrives at it in life—doesn't one?—with the sense of having had a revelation: one's personal past is a *place*, and everything that resides there does so in contemporaneous time. What then, of the collective past? The collective memory? That is where chronology really is. We come from the chaos of ourselves to the world, and we yearn to know what happened to all the others who came before us. So we impose Time on the flow of events, and call it history. For me, Memory is always *story*. True memory is nothing like the organized surface of a story, yet that is all we have to tell it, and know it, and experience it again: but if we are doomed to put our remembered life into stories, we are blessed by it, too.

I never spoke to my mother and father, or even to my brothers and sisters, about what I had seen at the funeral home. I don't know why, now. I can't recall why. Perhaps it was too private, finally; and perhaps I did not want to have it in memory, didn't want to fix it there in the telling. But it has never left me. It is with all the others, large and small, important and meaningless, all waiting in the same timeless dark, to drift toward the surface when I write, or daydream, or sleep.

A Book of Names

.   .   .   .

by
SYLVIA WATANABE

Recently I have caught myself, more often than I'd like, beginning sentences with the word *remember*. During one of our weekly phone conversations I told this to my father, who laughed. "I do that myself," he said; my father will turn eighty in October.

When I visit him in Honolulu we go for walks, just as we have always done. In the last several years these walks have become a ritual of naming what is there and no longer there—the koa grove, long since cut down, where we once found a blackburn butterfly; the ponds, where we looked for skimmers, now filled in and paved over. My father says, "If you live in a place long enough it begins to forget you."

My friend, Puanani, who lives in Wai'anae, which was once as rural as you could get, says that this forgetting has also spread there. Not long ago she ran into an old friend in the checkout line at their neighborhood mom-and-pop grocery. Her friend was looking around, distressed. She turned to Pua. "I was just realizing, I don't know a single person here," she said. "*And I never even moved.*"

When I left the island for graduate school and did not know I was leaving for good, I went to say good-bye to my grandmother, who lived with my mother's oldest sister.

"Don't go, there will be strangers there, you'll forget who you are," Grandmother said. This woman who, at the age of nineteen, divorced her husband in Japan, entered a paper marriage with a man she didn't know, sailed alone across the Pacific Ocean to a place she'd never seen, then spent the whole rest of her life remembering.

"But look at you, Obaasan," I reminded her. "You've never forgotten."

Grandmother waved me out the door. "Go then, go," she said, turning back to the television.

A year later she fell and broke her hip, and my aunt placed her in a facility for elderly care. At first Grandmother called home every day. "You have forgotten me here," she said.

Then she forgot where she was.

Forgetting comes to us inside our skins. I think of my uncle who forgot and forgot. As names came undone and slipped away, he forgot that a broom was not a tree, that the sky was not a sail. Desperate, my aunt thought to cure him with a health regimen. She put him on a special diet and fed him fish-oil capsules, said to be rich in memory substances. She took him for constitutionals on the beach, so he could take in the salt air. Sometimes he hummed, my aunt said, a kind of singsong; she could not make out the words. They sounded like either sea or she, forgets or forgives.

The sea, the sea where forgetting is.

My father finds refuge in the microcosm. By training and habit his gaze seeks out what is small. He says it gives you a different sense of time, the same sense you might get from looking at something vast.

When I was a child and he was late coming home from work, my mother never worried; she knew to send me only as far as the front yard, where I would find him lost between the front door and the garage, investigating the underside of a leaf or the creatures emerging from the cracks in the walk.

I remember her asking him once, dinner cold again, what he hoped to see, and he said, "Something I've never seen before."

The bookshelves in his study were filled with books naming all the things he'd seen and hadn't seen. In these books—he called them keys— were the names of rare and common insects, their habits and habitats and significance to human beings. On Saturday mornings, if there was nothing my mother needed us for, we packed the car with insect-collecting equipment and a box lunch of rice and salty Japanese pickles, then headed off to see something new.

On green days, smelling of fern, it rained on the mountain. Fern wings overhead, our gazes down, we hunted for damsels.

.   .   .   .

On gray summer days, swelling with heat, we searched for red dragonflies among the cattails.

On blue days at the edge of winter, the sky the color of pigment squeezed from a tube, we watched for *vanessas* among the mamaki.

My mother put up nicely with mosquito fish in her laundry tub, an earthworm farm, white mice, parakeets, an orphan lamb, cats, a dog, an escaped blue crab that lived three days behind the refrigerator before it died and began to stink, but she would not have jars of dead insects lying about her house. The one room where they were permitted was my father's study.

I sat next to him at his big desk, as he wrote out the labels for the new specimens we'd brought in. Slowly, meticulously, he printed the names: each letter a hieroglyph—a proboscis, a thorax, a pair of wings. When he was done he held up one of the labels he had written.

"*Vespidae*," he said.

I whispered it quickly for fear of getting stung.

"*Vespidae*," he repeated, laying down his pen. He taped the label he'd just written to the outside of the cigar box temporarily serving as a specimen case. Inside, rows of impaled wasps—black, iridescent blue, and gold—were suspended in flight, each anchored by a little tag naming genus and species, date and place of collection.

Carefully, my father tapped a couple more specimens out of the collecting jar. He picked one up with a pair of tweezers and pierced it clean through with a mounting pin. His hands dwarfed the delicate instruments; his movements were patient and precise. "Here," he said, pointing to a dangerous-looking yellow hornet, "you try it now." He sat while I gingerly retrieved it by a wing—which promptly detached itself. The other wing and two legs fell off as I wrestled the insect onto the pin. "There," I said. Without wings the hornet resembled a very large and angry ant. My father pointed out that this resemblance was no coincidence. Ants, wasps, and bees all belonged to the order, *hymenoptera*, an irritable, industrious bunch.

When my mother came to call us for dinner, I showed her my work. She looked thoughtful. "Ah, poor bee; he has been killed twice," she said.

If you know the name of a thing, you know what it is, my father believed. When I was eight, he gave me a clothbound notebook, with waterproof pages, like the one he carried everywhere. Here he kept a record of all the insects he'd observed with the details of their collection. If he did not know the name of an insect, he'd look it up later in one of his keys. On the outside of my notebook he had printed, A Book of Names.

As an entomologist for the Board of Health, it was my father's job to know the names of things. He supervised the inspectors who looked into the complaints of the public regarding infestations of various kinds. My father and his inspectors were responsible for finding where the trouble came from and getting rid of it. Although he's been retired nearly twenty years, this has been a habit that's proved hard to break. Now, when he comes to visit us in Michigan, he is the one to discover the termites in the woodpile, the ant trail in the mud room, the earwigs in the planter box next to the front door.

A few years ago, just after my husband and I started digging up the lawn and putting the perennial border in, I called my father, long-distance, to complain about something skeletonizing the *crambe cordefolia*. I could sense that he was tracing a familiar mental map, searching for a name. He had never seen a *crambe*; "What family does it belong to?" he asked. I couldn't say. He asked me to describe the physical characteristics of the plant, so I waxed aesthetic about the clouds of tiny flowers floating above the leaves on tall delicate stalks. There was a pause at his end, in which he did not remark how I had forgotten everything he'd ever taught me, but then he asked pointedly what the *leaves* were like. I described the large, abundant foliage, and after we'd discussed more specifically how the damage looked, he said it sounded as if the *crambe* were some kind of crucifer and that it was probably infested with caterpillars. He told me to go out at dark and check the undersides of the leaves. That evening, there they were: *plutella maculipennis*, dozens and dozens of green cabbage worms feeding.

Popillia japonica, vanessa tameamea, megabombus pennsylvanicus. These are the names my father taught me. I pictured the names as fasteners, like specimen pins, holding what we could not hold in our hands: red hibiscus afternoons, crickets ringing in the grass, the rain smell rising from a forest floor. I loved to say the names aloud, to hear the magic sound of them.

My father spoke of their precision. "They are like points on a map," he said. Order, family, genus, species: They followed a path. It was always the same path; the path was a story. You are mine now, the story said. You are not strange to me anymore.

. . . .

Recently I told this to my father, who thought it over a moment, then said, "If you've seen one bug you've seen them all, I guess."

I remember reading somewhere that the Hawaiian language classifies insects under a different scheme—according to whether they are big or small, creeping or flying, burrowing or wood-boring, biting or not biting. The language pays a great deal of attention to other animals—for example, to birds and birdcatching techniques, fish and the places in the sea to find fish, but it does not pay much attention to naming bugs.

Of much greater import are the names attached to human beings. Puanani Burgess, my friend from Wai'anae who is a storyteller and poet, says that according to traditional Hawaiian belief, a person's essence inheres in a name. A name might include the place and conditions of birth, ancestral lineage, traditional family occupations, and the particular form of *mana*—or spiritual power—possessed by a line. Sometimes names can run very long. The full name of Mary Kawena Pukui, a famous native cultural historian, was Mary Abigail Kawena-'ula-o-ka-lani-a-Hi'iaka-i-ka-poli-o-Pele-ka-wahine-'ai-honua Na-lei-lehua-a-Pele Wiggin, which translated meant, "The rosy glow in the sky made by Hi'iaka in the bosom of Pele, the earth-consuming woman. The crimson lehua wreaths of Pele."

A name can bring good or bad luck. If bad fortune comes, the name and the memories that adhere to it are "cut away," or removed, with offerings and prayers. This is a practice that might have seemed familiar to my Japanese grandmother, who told me once that my aunt Tsune, with whom she lived, had not always been called Tsune. At birth she had been named Hayako, but she had been an especially difficult child—crying and fussing and nothing could make her stop. Finally at wit's end Grandmother consulted a fortune-teller who told her that the child had been given the wrong name. The fortune-teller said that the Chinese character for Hayako meant, among other things, to precipitate, which helped to bring on the crying fits. The baby needed a name that would counter her temperament. The fortune-teller chose Tsune, as a pun on the verb, tsumeru, which means to plug. "Perhaps I went too far," Grandmother admitted. "Now, when she is angry, she will not speak."

Puanani's poem, "Choosing My Name," can be read as a kind of name-changing rite in the Hawaiian tradition. In this poem she describes how she was given three names—*Christabelle*, *Yoshie*, and *Puanani*—and how she has come to decide among them. She says *Christabelle* was her name for school and church and belongs to a life now left behind, while *Yoshie* has come to signify her Japanese father's family and their sometimes only grudging acceptance, but it is *Puanani*, the name given her by her Hawaiian mother, that binds her to the land and to the wholeness of a life becoming forgotten.

My father does not imagine things in quite these terms, but for him, as well, the memory of place exerts a kind of somatic pull. Several years ago my husband and I took a trip with my father to Maui, where he grew up. Although he hadn't been back in many years, he never got lost. Progress had occurred almost everywhere we went, but he could see through what was there to what no longer was—the sites of disappeared sugar villages, the mountain routes he'd hiked as a boy, the best places along the shoreline for torching, throwing net, casting, and spearing. He showed us where he'd harvested honey from the wild bee hives in the kiawe pasture and looked for hawk moths among the be-still trees. He pointed out where he'd gone fishing off Kipahulu the night before the tidal wave and caught nothing but sharks. Speeding down the narrow hilly road to Ulapalakoa, he searched for shortcuts, no longer there, back down to the low country. It seemed he had walked, climbed, fished, swum, driven almost every inch of the island—the memory of it like a map imprinted on skin.

"I remember," my father says, and the names open like windows. I have stepped into his nostalgia so many times, it almost seems mine, but I have never known a place in just that way. Since our early walks, I have come to see names in a different light—although I guess you could say I still collect them.

Often over the past ten years, I've wondered if maybe my grandmother's worst fears haven't come true and I haven't turned into somebody, or somebodies, else. At various times I have been Sylvia, or Cynthia, or Celia Wanatabe, Wan*tan*abe, *Wan*tanabe, Wabatabe, Whatabobby, Whatanade—my names choose me. They shift from day to day, moment to moment, depending on whether I'm talking to the mail-order lady at L.L. Bean or the man behind the counter at the local post office. Lately, even my husband has begun receiving solicitations in the mail addressed to William P. Osbornabe.

I have gotten used to inquiries over the telephone as to whether my name is "Indian," or "African," or "Eskimo." Once, just after we moved to Grand Rapids, I went to a doctor I had never been to before. I could hear him, rustling papers outside the examining-room door. When he fi-

. . . .

nally came in, he paused, a look of amazement on his face. "Why you're not Polish," he exclaimed. "Not even close," I said. He had been trying to figure out my name from the medical file, and not being Polish himself, he said, that was the best he could come up with.

Another time, when I was trying to make a dental appointment by telephone, I gave my name to the receptionist, who was new. She asked—as I'd learned to expect, "What kind of name is that, where're you from?" When I told her Hawaii, she grew enthusiastic. "Well, Miss . . . miss . . . miss Wannabe, welcome to America!" she said.

On bad days, I wonder which name is causing the trouble. If I could get people not to call me Ms. Whatabee for a while, would my luck improve? And how would I go about doing that? It seems the method of my grandmother's fortune-teller would work only if all parties agreed on what your name was and what it wasn't. I do not think anymore that a name is a kind of fastener that holds memory in place. Even now as I write, the signifiers are emptying out and refilling, changing shape, becoming something else. I find myself imagining the Polish African Indian Eskimo Sylvia Wampumabee and how she might tell this.

Nostalgia is memory looking off to one side. Any minute that thing you're not looking at might slide into view. Remember, my father says, or I say— but there is a place between now and before where we do not go. This is what we want to forget: Grandmother in the ambulance, Uncle empty of names.

When my mother became ill, the doctors could not name what was wrong. There was no map, no path to follow. They could say what her symptoms were like—they were like arthritis. Physical therapy was prescribed. We didn't know, till much later, it was her liver that failed her.

For months after she died, my father left everything as it was. Her footsteps whispering through the rooms, her breath in the air, her sleep still warming the unchanged sheets. He went about his day's routine as if she were the reason—waking when it was still dark in the windows, fixing six tiny meals of her favorite foods. He went for a walk some mornings, then cleaned house in the afternoons to her favorite soap operas; he couldn't say what was going on, but the sounds from the television belonged in the air. You get used to things, he said. And while he might, in time, become used to something else (he avoided the words, *absence*, *death*), it was not yet that time.

.   .   .   .

Meanwhile, stacks of old newspapers collected in the hall. He collected beer bottles, cans, jars of all sizes (in case, as he said, he took up pickling), the cardboard tubes from rolls of toilet paper, two stray cats. He collected flotsam the way he once collected butterflies. All the items were organized by size and type—paper goods here, metal there—except the cats, who had the habit of wandering off.

A few months after the funeral, I was back visiting and we were sitting in the living room drinking beers. I said to my father, "What's all this, Pop? This is a firetrap, throw something out."

He gazed at the neatly sorted piles of this and that, then laughed. "These are the days of our lives," he said. "These are the days of our lives."

The signifiers are shifting.
The world is becoming unpinned.

My father and I have added forgetting walks to our repertoire. A forgetting walk happens when you walk into a room and do not remember why you are there. Or when you can't get past the fifth word of the sentence, "The other day I saw—now who was that—you know, what was her name, it was just there on the tip of my tongue. . . ." Or just before you are about to leave the house, perhaps to go on another kind of walk, when one of you remembers you have forgotten something. You wander from room to room, calling out, "Where are my glasses? Where are my keys?"

While she was in the senior-care facility, my grandmother went on her own naming walks. In the evening, after supper, she'd wheel down the hall, stopping at each doorway and putting her hands together in prayer. This annoyed some of the inhabitants who shouted rude things, but Grandmother continued, undeterred. Her last stop was the visitors' lounge, where she wheeled up to the refrigerator and pulled the doors open, just as she'd opened the doors of the tabletop shrine at home. Then she'd chant loudly into that cold white space, a single word, the Buddha's name over and over again.

Lately everyone in Hawaii is changing names; talk of Sovereignty fills the air. There's Richard, the sansei poet, who now performs Hawaiian reggae liberation rap under the name of Red Flea. Then there's Diana, the novelist, who's become Kiana. And Carolyn Lau who has turned into Carolyn

. . . .

Lei-Lanilau. And Dennis who did not change his name but spent an afternoon getting an ankle tatooed in the traditional native Hawaiian manner.

I tell my father, who doesn't quite know what to make of all this, that he must also pick out a name for when the revolution comes. He says that he already has one; he read it in the paper the other day. In an interview someone called local "orientals" *neocolonialists*.

"I guess that's your name too," my father says.

Forgetting is remembering.
I remember forgetting.

The scent of the night garden comes to me. The darkness brimming with the sweetness of honeysuckle, pikake, night-blooming cereus—the creamy white blooms in the silver light. My father carries the net—it is long and deep, narrowing at the end like a magician's hat. I can see my mother through the kitchen window, she is washing dishes at the sink. She looks up and peers out, but cannot see us in the dark. She is beautiful in the yellow light.

My father passes the net once over the flower bed and a winged form appears in it. Army worm moth, drab little sister. He waves his net again and produces a flying cockroach. One more pass, and a gray sphinx materializes. This is it, my father says.

We take the moth into the light. My mother sees us now. "Don't you let that loose in here," she calls through the screen.

My father turns the net inside out, and the moth clings to the fine mesh, curiously still. I have never seen one like this before. It has a furry body, large red-jeweled eyes and a coiled nose—like a pincurl. My father explains that this is not really a nose, but a proboscis, which is a kind of straw for sipping nectar. The moth's wings are slightly open, and they are light grey—almost silver—and covered with delicate patterns of grey, darker grey, black, and white. I brush my fingers against them and they flutter a little. They feel like air.

The Third Servant

. . . .

by

MARGOT LIVESEY

In the small Dutch village of Goes where my first lover grew up, the tradi-tional dress for women is a short-sleeved blouse that reveals the biceps, polished on special occasions with red wax until they shine like apples. If there is a Mount Olympus where the gods keep house, I like to think that Mnemosyne must be polishing her biceps vigourously these days, flashing them at such lowly beings as Aphrodite and Zeus and Pluto. Although her ambiguities and uncertainties are well documented, she has become an unquestioned good, in the forefront of court cases, books, conversations; even the vexed topic of repressed memory is only another aspect of homage. Meanwhile her dark sister, amnesia, is viewed with suspicion and fear: a harbinger of senility, evidence of trauma or, at the very least, a sign of transgression. That which we do not remember, we are doomed to repeat.

Here is something I do remember. In a pew near the front of the church, I swung my legs, too short to reach the floor, and listened to Mr. Chisolm, director of the Sunday school, expound on the parable of the talents. This was in the village of Denholm in the Borders of Scotland where we lived for five years. The church was built of the local grey granite and, in the presiding spirit of John Knox, very plain; the only decorations were the memorial windows. Mr. Chisolm too was a man without adornment. His large face, from collarline to hairline, was a muted strawberry colour, ditto his large hands. He favoured a brown suit. He and his wife lived a few houses away from us and he ran a greengrocer's. As a delivery boy, he told the Sunday school, he had carried a Bible in his pocket at all times; we should do the same.

. . . .

Now he repeated the parable. A man, going into a far country, hands over his goods to his servants for safekeeping. He gives five talents to one servant, two to another, one to another. The first two servants trade and double their money; the third buries his single talent in the ground. When the master returns he applauds the first two and reproaches the third.

> Thou wicked and slothful servant, thou knewest that I reap where I sowed not, and gather where I have not strawed. . . . Take therefore the talent from him, and give it unto him which hath ten talents. For unto every one that hath shall be given, and he shall have abundance: but from him that hath not shall be taken away even that which he hath.

The talents, Mr. Chisolm explained, were God's gifts to us which, as good Christians, we must use to our utmost. Failure to do so, he tut-tutted, was a sin. I don't know how the other children felt, hearing his stern comments, but I yearned to defend the third servant. Was it really so wrong to hang on to what one had been given? To take care of what one had got?

Several centuries before Jesus, Plato, in the *Theaetetus*, offers various theories of knowledge. "Now let us make in each soul a sort of aviary of all kinds of birds; some in flocks separate from the others, some in small groups, and others flying about singly here and there among all the rest." He goes on to argue that just as a man can be said to have these birds, at the same time he doesn't exactly have them; he still has to catch them and in doing so may easily mistake the ringdove for the pigeon. What better metaphor for the odd relationship we have with our own memories.

I was eight the year I sat listening to Mr. Chisolm. My father, who had tested me on the parable before I went to Sunday school, was fifty-seven. We were both of us much more familiar with Thanatos, the ultimate taker away, than with abundance although my father had always managed to get what he needed. He was born in 1904, three years after the death of Queen Victoria, the same year as Cecil Beaton and Christopher Isherwood. His birth, following the death of a beloved older brother, was surrounded by threats: childbirth might prove fatal to my grandmother; a third pregnancy was out the question. Between the dead and the unborn my father slipped into the world and assumed his burden of affection. He was christened John for his brother, Kenneth for himself, Livesey for his father and known variously as Kenneth, Toby, and Silas. Later he took the place of another dead boy; one of my grandfather's parishioners paid his fees at first public school, then Cambridge University, in memory of a son who had died early in the Great War.

For the two decades before we moved to Denholm my father had been teaching at Glenalmond, a well-known boys' public school north of Edinburgh. On every possible occasion he had been passed over for promotion. Then, frighteningly close to retirement, he was lured south by Mr. Case, the charismatic owner of a prep school called Blenearne. What Mr. Case offered was the title of vice headmaster and the chance to continue teaching—arithmetic, geography and religious education—for as long as my father wanted. My stepmother, a former nurse, would be the assistant matron and we would live in the nearby village.

Saint Augustine in his *Confessions* was among the first to pay homage at Mnemosyne's altar. Memory, he writes, is a crucial stage on our journey to God; he puzzles over its immensity. "All these sensations are retained in the great storehouse of the memory, which in some indescribable way secretes them in its folds." It is, he concludes, a faculty not of the mind but of the soul.

Like so many private schools at that time, Blenearne was based in a country house. Prospective parents were seduced by the beautiful drawing room and velvety lawns. Also by Casey himself, not so much a devoted educationalist as a swashbuckling buccaneer, complete with a dashing moustache and mysterious past. A mysterious present too. No one quite knew how he balanced the books or where the money for new buildings came from—stables, a tennis court, a games room—but who cared when he served such good sherry and had such excellent manners.

Years later, thinking I might write a novel about my father, I researched the phenomenon of British private schools. In the nineteenth century, I discovered, boys at Harrow and Eton could not even count on having their own beds; the great hall at Eton, locked after supper each evening, was a world unto itself where no adult dared enter; up through the First World War intellectual accomplishments were discounted if not actively discouraged. As for the many smaller private schools that orbited these historic institutions, they seem to have been an unlicensed free-for-all. Anyone who could get his hands on a large house was able to start one. Of course I mean any middle-class man who had to earn a living and felt himself ill-suited for the army or the church. My father, prior to his stint at Glenalmond, was involved in starting two prep schools, each of which went bust and which together lost him most of his mother's money. In some ways Blenearne must have felt like coming home.

When I finally visited my grandfather's church in the Lake District, a decade after my father's death, I found it even smaller than the one in Denholm and just as plain. Like his son, my grandfather, Samuel, had been passed over for preferment. My grandmother, Florence, who chain-smoked, wore a cloak and hairpiece and said whatever came into her head, was not considered a good wife for a vicar. Rather than scaling the church hierarchy, Samuel was given the impoverished living of Skels-mergh. His former parishioners, the few I spoke to, all agreed what a nice man he was and very learned but oh dear, his sermons were dull. Then they went on to tell yet another story about the redoubtable Florence.

In his classic *Matter and Memory* (1910), the French philospher Henri Bergson claims that while animals are capable of a certain kind of memory, a dog recognises his master, only humans have the knack of withdrawing, uselessly, from the present moment into the past.

> Man alone is capable of such an effort. But even in him the past to which he returns is fugitive, ever on the point of escaping him, as though his backward-turning memory were thwarted by the other, more natural memory, of which the forward movement bears him on to action and to life.

My father must have gone to Sunday school and church weekly throughout his boyhood and at the various schools he attended, as pupil or teacher, prayers were held once, often twice, a day. Was he a Christian in any meaningful sense? I couldn't say but for whatever reason when we moved to Denholm, I became the sole churchgoer in the family. Mr. Waugh, the minister, shared my grandfather's gift for tedious sermons; he also had a difficult wife, in his case not flamboyant but, according to village gossip, mad. They lived in a house shadowed by monkey puzzle trees and she was never seen. From my years of services I recall a single occasion; one winter morning, during Mr. Waugh's mumbled prayer, someone in a nearby pew began to cut their nails. I counted, wondering if the clicks would go past ten.

What did my father and stepmother do during the two hours I spent at Sunday school and church? Answer: enjoyed my absence. In addition perhaps they did a crossword puzzle or went for a drive to see the racehorses who lived on the far side of the river. Perhaps they watched our newly rented television, although I'm not certain there were programmes on Sunday morning. When I returned from my devotions, did we eat lunch together or did I, as usual, eat first, alone, while they had a glass of sherry? I don't remember but suspect the latter.

The most famous of mnemonic devices is of no help in such matters. The invention of memory palaces was at one time attributed to Cicero, the

Roman orator. In fact the notion seems to have cropped up in several places in the first century B.C. and the first century A.D.. Pliny, Quintilian, and the anonymous author of *Ad Herennium* all write about using buildings and images to hold onto memory.

The idea was a simple one. The orator chose different images—striking, ugly, beautiful—to assign to the different parts of his speech and placed these images in the rooms of a familiar building; he had then only to imagine himself walking through it in order to retrieve his speech. Of course if no suitable building were available that was a problem; rhetoric students were sometimes observed pacing the forum, memorising it, pillar by pillar.

The use and practise of palaces peaked in the sixteenth century with hyperelaborate structures and gradually fell out of favour. Jonathan D. Spence in his wonderful book *The Memory Palace of Matteo Ricci* describes how when the Jesuit missionary Matteo Ricci tried to introduce the idea into China, the governor's eldest son remarked that one needed a very good memory to make use of his advice. And that is probably how the notion strikes most of us today, cumbersome and faintly comic but 1,600 years is a good innings for any theory.

Not only the palaces per se but also the feats they facilitated have fallen into disrepute. We value memory, for rather different reasons, as highly as Augustine did but the rote memory, so beloved of Mr. Chisolm and the schoolteachers of my father's generation, has fallen out of favour; W. H. Auden was considered fuddy-duddy for making his American students learn poems by heart. My father was blessed with a good memory for the mathematical equations and formulae of his profession. As for the other kind of memory, who knows? He almost never spoke of the past, save for a handful of well-honed stories. Of course, I never asked.

In our century the favourite mnemonic device is probably the photograph. The few I have inherited of my father show a beautiful boy and a handsome young man with fair, wavy hair, clear skin, a mouth suggesting both pride and sensitivity and, as several people reported to me, lovely bright blue eyes. Auden might have fancied him, Isherwood too; I have no idea if he had inclinations that way. In my lifetime one of his few close friends, another master at Glenalmond, was gay, although of course this was never referred to. As Oscar Wilde's situation makes clear much that today we insist on naming, then went unnamed. Perhaps my father was a rent boy; perhaps he was victimised by older boys; perhaps he sought younger boys. Who knows?

Certainly not Godfrey Clapham, his former roommate at Shrewsbury School. At the age of eighty-four Godfrey made the perilous journey from suburban Sydenham into central London in response to a letter I had sent to my father's few surviving fellow pupils. In the buffet at Victoria Station, amidst travellers and panhandlers, he explained that they had shared a study. I gazed in wonder at his watery eyes and knobbly hands; here was the man who could deliver my young father to me, break through that half century of silence. What was he like? I asked. A nice chap, said Godfrey, quiet. Did you like him? Yes, yes I think so. Did he have hobbies? I remember him, Godfrey insisted, voice rising and, before I could press him further, began to reminisce about the school food, especially bad from 1916 to 1918.

Later, when I returned with a second pot of tea, he produced from his brown plastic shopping bag proof of his claim: a photograph of the School House at Shrewsbury in 1917. Godfrey himself, long-faced, is standing near the centre of the group, straining slightly as if he must see in order to be seen. My father on the far left, near the railings, is out of focus.

Most of the men who responded to my letter, and nearly everyone who was still alive did answer, either in quavering handwriting or shouting into the phone, turned out to use the word "remember" in Godfrey's sense. They remembered my father, that he had existed, that they had known him, but when I showed up to question them they did not, it transpired, remember anything about him. Instead they talked happily about themselves.

What does make us remember one thing rather than another? A writer friend said if you had a use for your memories, you would remember them. Not so. Not yet. Half Godfrey's age, most of my schoolfellows have already vanished from my mind. If I should live so long will they return?

In *The Mind of a Mnemonist* the Russian psychologist A. R. Luria portrays a man with a limitless memory. The mnemonist, instinctively, uses the theories of *Ad Herennium*, distributing objects, numbers, words along streets and in buildings he knows. On one occasion, when he actually seems to forget something, he offers the following explanation.

> I put the image of the pencil near a fence. . . . but what happened was that the image fused with that of the fence and I walked right on past without noticing it. The same thing happened with the word egg. I had put it up against a white wall and it blended with the background.

By the time we left Glenalmond my father and I had already had several encounters with Thanatos. In May of 1951 his mother, Florence, who had spent her decade of widowhood cheerfully bossing him around, died. On the first of August 1952 he married the school nurse, Eva; perhaps not incidentally she too had recently lost her sole surviving parent, her father. I was born the following year. Two and a half years later, Eva disappeared. For weeks and months I asked for her only to be told she had gone shopping. "My mummy's gone to buy me sweeties," I explained to whoever would listen. Eventually someone broke down and told me she was dead. A year and a half after that my father remarried and Little Aunt, who had cared for me since Eva's death, also disappeared. She went to live with her older sister in Edinburgh, a mere fifty miles away but, to my four-year-old self, not yet a letter writer or reader, a kind of death. We did not have a phone.

In the midst of these disappearances some constants remained. As a boy my father climbed the hills in search of peregrine falcons, and he passed on to me his feeling for nature. I woke to the cawing of rooks in the rookery beside our house. Geese veed the sky each autumn. In the spring baby swallows squalked in their nests outside my bedroom window and tadpoles spawned in the stream at the bottom of the golf course. I knew where to find the first primroses and later the delicate Star of David. More than all this I had companionship. Our neighbours with four children left their door open for me from breakfast 'til bedtime. Then we moved to Denholm and I was the one who died.

In *Searching for Memory* Daniel Schacter draws the distinction between field and observer memories, those memories in which we see ourselves and those in which we see only what we saw. Childhood memories, he claims, are more likely to be field memories. He goes on to discuss how memories can sometimes be flipped from one state to the other and how doing so changes the emotional charge. I try to picture my younger self— climbing a tree or finding a bat that had flown into the bike shed—but as far as I can tell, I have no field memories. I see the tree trunk, the bat's tiny ears, the people around me, never myself. When I try the result is a blur, a fleeting image. Was that me? I can't be sure.

My father at the time of our move was still a good-looking man, capable of charm and humour, quick to laugh at a joke, an excellent mimic. People I interviewed, those who praised his beautiful eyes, also commented on his yellow teeth but to me his dentures, like his nicotine-stained fingers, only made him more interesting. His suits, he wore one every day, were not yet threadbare. Nevertheless he and my stepmother failed to make friends. She, who had grown up in a small croft in the north of Scot-

. . . . , .

land, regarded the village people as common. As for the other masters at Blenearne, I don't know why but none ever darkened our door. Even if they had made friends, it wouldn't have helped me; they would only have been more middle-aged people smoking and talking and drinking over my head. Without our neighbours, the birds, the familiar landscape, the shape of our family became sharply apparent, like a tree in winter.

No one yet knows exactly how memory works, what forms it, what summons it, what obliterates it. One of the many anomalies is that memory often becomes detached from its source, as in the famous case of Freud proposing to Fliess that every person is fundamentally bisexual, only to have Fliess respond that he had suggested this to Freud two years before. Looking through the notes I made nearly a decade ago while interviewing people about my father I find the following list: cricket, bonfire, shiatsu. Neither memory nor source follows.

The list of things my father and I did not do is much longer than the one of those we did. We did not talk or play or, in Denholm, go for walks. He did not help with my homework because he had to supervise his pupils and by the time he came home I was on my way to bed. He did not visit the farm on the outskirts of the village where I went daily, nor did he help with the grocery shopping, my Saturday morning chore. Our main activities together were horticultual; we weeded the garden and picked black currants or gooseberries. He did stop the village boys from throwing stones at me, by speaking to their headmaster. And once, astonishingly, he intervened with my stepmother. She had called me a slut, I was nine, because I hadn't cleaned my room properly and he said something to the effect that, like him, I was not naturally tidy.

The degree to which questioning distorts memory is now well-documented but priming, overt or subtle, is often crucial to remembrance. What I suffered from as an interviewer was precisely the condition I was seeking to remedy: how little I knew my father. I did not know what questions to ask Godfrey and the others, to bring back that blue-eyed boy.

Perhaps because of our solitude we never spent the holidays in Denholm. At Christmas we went to visit Little Aunt in Edinburgh and in the summers we went to the town of Pitlochry in the Highlands to stay with my stepmother's sister. There, sometimes, my father and I would walk the dog in the Recreation Ground until she was put to sleep, the year I turned ten. We did go to the library together where I looked for books about adventure and he chose genteel murder stories for himself and my stepmother. Once or twice he accompanied me to the putting green, which was run by a former groundsman from Glenalmond. Most of the time though I tapped a ball round the twelve holes alone.

The originator of the memory palace, the first practitioner, is said to be the Greek poet, Simonides. At a banquet Simonides recited a poem to the applause of the other guests. His patron, however, meanly declared that he would pay only for the portion of the poem about him. A few minutes later a servant brought word that Simonides was wanted ouside. While he was talking to two men, in some versions of the story Castor and Pollux, the roof of the hall collapsed, killing everyone. Simonides identified the mangled bodies not by clothes or jewellery but by remembering the seating order. Surely it can be no coincidence that even here memory is inextricably linked to death.

I doubt my father ever went to a banquet; I know he never boarded a plane. He was successful in neither his business ventures nor his teaching. Like his parents, he lived in rented or tied accommodation his entire life and, during the years we lived together, he did not buy a new car nor a new suit but he was beloved by three women: his mother, my mother, his second wife. A fourth name ought to appear on this list but I cannot say with confidence that it does.

A few months ago, driving from Edinburgh to the west coast of Scotland, I passed a sign, Rannoch Moor, 1,700 Feet. Into my head, unbidden, came the sentence: This was where my father nearly died. As far as the eye could see were heather, rocks, bogs, not a tree in sight.

When I was thirteen something wonderful happened. My school, the school I hated, closed down and my parents arranged for me to return to Glenalmond and live with our former neighbours. The happiness that attended these events is indescribable. Days passed without my giving my parents a thought, save during the composition of my weekly letter and the reading of my father's replies, witty accounts of his and my stepmother's small doings. I had not heard his voice for almost two months when he phoned to announce that Blenearne, too, was closing. At the age of sixty-two, already struggling with emphysema, he was out of a job and homeless. My stepmother went to Pitlochry to live with her sister and he took a substitute job at Rannoch School. Sometime that spring the cold dampness of the moor brought on bronchitis that turned into pneumonia.

My stepmother nursed him back to health and he carried on for nine more years to die as his father had done, of a sudden heart attack, the autumn I was twenty-two. Until recently I would have bet serious money that I did not attend his funeral but soon after my journey across Rannoch

Moor, I found myself telling a friend, yet again, the story of his death. How I was at the opposite end of the country, staying in a remote Cornish village, when I heard the news. How I sat on a windy station platform, waiting for the train that would take me to London where I could catch the sleeper north. So you didn't get back to Scotland in time, she said gently.

A wall, a cloud, a tangle of leaves rose before me. The journey took twenty-four hours. I was in Scotland in time for the funeral. If I was there, then I must have attended. Quod erat demonstrandum: I was present that day when all that remained of my father, my last living relative, disappeared into the flames.

And?

And nothing. No memory follows my deduction, not even a shadow, hovering on the tip of my tongue, only a white pool of forgetfulness.

Schacter quotes research which indicates that people remember sad information more accurately when in a sad mood. Would the day return if I reread *The Little Mermaid*, which always used to make me cry? If I went back to Perth Crematorium, or spoke to people who were present that day and had not themselves forgotten, who could tell me what hymns were sung, what prayers were said? Would I at least start to recall, like Godfrey, that I was present even if I remembered nothing about the occasion? Perhaps. But for now forgetfulness seems more powerful, more peculiarly informative, than any memory.

My father finished out the year at Rannoch and got a job in the boys' half of the girls' school I attended. My life as a commuter began. He and my stepmother rented a farmhouse and I spent the weekdays there in a small L-shaped bedroom; every Friday I went back to Glenalmond. For two years the main time I saw my father alone was during our drives to and from the school. I don't remember us talking, only him hunching forward anxiously, again and again, to wipe the windscreen. Around that time I read *King Lear* and discovered one of his favourite quotations, "Oh, sharper than a serpent's tooth to have a thankless child." He said it often, joking I assumed.

In class, of course, I sided with the frustrating Cordelia but outside I was firmly in the camp of Goneril and Regan. The only way I could bear the shame of my father's decrepit car, worn clothes, and terrible teaching was by joining in the taunts against him. At my previous school I had been so desperate to avoid my classmates that I hid in the school cloakroom or cut myself with the blade of my pencil sharpener so as to have an excuse to go and see the school nurse; I was determined not to let the same fate befall me here.

For both of us his retirement, at the age of sixty-five, came not a moment too soon. As years before I had gone to church alone, now I went to school, rising, often in darkness, to lay the fire, breakfast, and walk down the muddy track to catch the bus. What my father and my stepmother did all day I have no notion, pottered their way through the rituals of meals and drinks, crossword puzzles and television, exclaiming over the birds who visited the feeder, the comings and goings at the farm. I came home at 4:30 to do my homework. At 7:30 they summoned me to supper. At last I was allowed to eat with them.

One of the most pervasive myths about memory, and Saint Augustine must be partly responsible for this, is that everything is retained. We may not be able to gain access but it's all there somewhere, the whole mess of daily life: the tedium, the horror, the anxiety, the joy. Against this science offers the sharp curve of forgetting. In half an hour, research suggests, we forget 90 percent of what we experience. The 10 percent that remains will probably stay with us for much longer.

Was this what I had craved? To sit around the mahogany-veneer table and endure my stepmother's complaints that my father and I were not eating enough. And worse, much worse, the laboured conversation. Boring, stupid, I chanted to myself, dull, bourgeois. Surely I must have understood this was the effect of my presence? As rapidly as possible, I cleared the table, washed the dishes and, leaving my parents to the television, returned to my homework. Soon after the nine o'clock news they called good night to me and climbed the stairs to bed. It would not have occurred to me to wonder what they did there. I am the only evidence I have of my father's sex life.

Since the death of my stepmother's brother-in-law, Thanatos had been neglecting us. Now Little Aunt came to stay from Edinburgh. At first she seemed her usual self, always glad to see me, but day by day she stayed in bed longer, rose from her armchair with more reluctance, had no appetite even for her favourite cough sweets. One afternoon, arriving home from school, I went to her room and found her asleep but not asleep. Her face had changed, her nose sharpened, cheeks hollowed. Her breathing was loud and strange. I crept into her room several times, fascinated, afraid. Something was happening; I had no idea what. My parents simply said she was under the weather and dispatched me to Glenalmond. Next day my father phoned with the news Little Aunt was dead. She was only in her early seventies but no one mentioned a cause. Once again I have no memory of the funeral. At sixteen, I may or may not have attended.

Little Aunt left a will naming me the heir to her small store of wordly goods, my father her executor. All his life he had done what women told him. Now he did my stepmother's bidding, honouring the verbal bequests she claimed Little Aunt had made in her final weeks. If she had lived, my stepmother explained to me, she would have changed her will. She couldn't believe how badly you'd turned out: spoiled, rude, lazy.

I know little of my father's last four years. I finished school, I went to university. When I asked him for the parental contribution to my grant, he refused, arguing that I could always come home during the holidays. He wrote to me at university, making little silk purses out of his and my stepmother's dull days. I hope I wrote back. When I did pay one of my rare visits home he also wrote to me, coming into the room where I worked to place on the table an envelope bearing my name. How I wish now I had kept those letters. Alas, as soon as I figured out that no response was required, I destroyed them. The last time I saw my father alive, after a year abroad, such a letter passed between us. Like all the hand-delivered missives, his final words expressed disappointment at my conduct.

In my pew at Denholm I recognised the third servant's situation but only in material terms; if you already had a ten-speed bicycle, you would probably get a pony. It took me years to grasp that this was an account of the spiritual, the psychological, not of bank balances and careers. If security and happiness are among your early companions, there's a good chance they will continue to be so. But if despair and difficulty rock your cradle, they may show an unfortunate tendency to take up permanent residence in your household. "From him that hath not shall be taken away even that which he hath."

Cricket, bonfire, shiatsu. Mnemosyne, Thanatos, Eros. In all our lives these three dance attendance. One is banished for a while, then another, but never for long. In the old stories it is Eros who defeats Thanatos, who goes down into the underworld and returns triumphant. Now, in our secular century, Mnemosyne seems to offer our main hope against Thanatos and who knows this better than those of us who were given only a single talent.

If I were to make a memory palace for my father, then I would use one of our schools, not Blenearne of which all save his classroom has blurred, nor Rannoch which I never knew, maybe Morrison's Academy for Girls. Between the double entrance doors I'd put my father, squatting, oblivious to the lengthening ash of his cigarette, telling with gusto some story he had told before, perhaps the one about his mother in the hospital, unable to get the nurse's attention, throwing a plate of biscuits at the door. Outside the headmistress's office, I'd put him on the golf course at Glenalmond, playing the number two hole, squinting into the sun, pleading with the ball as it winged its way down the fairway. In the school gym with its dangling ropes and vaulting boxes, I'd put his endless devotion to my stepmother. How happy he was to have a woman, another woman, who both adored him and was always ready to tell him what to do. In the library where I read from A to Z, I'd put what I do remember from the time of his death.

A few weeks after my father's fatal heart attack, one overcast morning, I was driving his car along the main road, the journey we had made twice a day to and from Morrison's Academy, when I spotted something on the tarmac ahead. I stopped and went to kneel beside the wounded partridge. There were no other travellers, only the sough of wind in the pine trees, no blood on its tawny plumage; clearly the partridge had suffered a blow from an earlier vehicle. When I reached for it, the bird was too weak to resist. In my hands its heart beat with eerie speed, and I knew by the filming of its eyes that death was near. All the country lore of my childhood told me I ought to put it out of its misery. But as I moved toward the verge a movement caught my eye. In the long grass half a dozen other partridges were bobbing and clucking. The bird was not alone; the rest of the covey were trying to draw me off, distract me, save it. I set the warm bird down in the grass, close to its companions, and drove away.

Don't Look

.   .   .   .

by
VICTORIA MORROW

When we were children, my older brother Michael trained me to not look at him. For most of our lives together he would beat me mercilessly if I ever met his eyes. If he caught me looking—even at his shoes—he would growl two words, "Don't look," then dive on me and punch me hard—in the back, in the arm, in the chest. For years he was my worst enemy. I was terrified of him. He didn't want me to look at him and I didn't. I never looked.

Michael held a deep, particular hatred for me. He beat me up much more brutally and more often than either of my other brothers did. His fury was deep, unfathomable, relentless. There was no logic as to what would set him off. I was Michael's special victim, the youngest, the easiest prey. I would not put up a fight as my other siblings would have. My only defense was in trying to keep physical barriers between us: when Michael got that look on his face, that rage, I'd run into my room and lean all my weight against my bedroom door, waiting until he'd throw himself against the other side. Michael broke door frames, splintered doors around the hinges, to get in at me. I developed little tricks to keep the door closed for a few seconds longer, like shoving a plastic comb into the corner of the door frame, but they didn't keep Michael at bay for very long. He always succeeded in getting in at me. Sometimes he came armed with a kitchen knife or other weapon, which for some reason my mother thought was funny. Maybe she thought he was kidding around. I know he was not. The whole thing, the chase, the beating, was a game for Michael, a challenge. He was never thwarted by obstacles, only encouraged. And my mother never rebuked him.

Michael had always been the sick child, coddled and made allowances for. My mother gave him special attention: he had asthma and epilepsy, and his epileptic seizures were bad. He was reliant on medication, and his senses were dulled from the Dilantin and phenobarbital. He could drop anywhere, and did. People in school kept their distance. No one knew what to do when he checked out, first with the vacant look then the sudden twitching, then the fall to the floor with eyes rolling, mouth foaming. If the seizure happened at home, we had directions—hold his head, try to prevent him from choking on his tongue, then let him thrash it out—sit back and observe the grand mal electrocution on the kitchen floor. Observe. Michael was aware of what a sideshow he was, and he hated it. He didn't want to be noticed, didn't want to be looked at. Michael hated being chosen by my mother as the special child. It made him different from the rest of us, and that difference made him angry. He hated himself so he beat me.

For years I omitted these beatings from my past. I didn't want to remember them, and so I didn't. My childhood, if anyone asked, was fine, thanks. There were five of us kids and I was the youngest. My parents had been divorced since I was eight months old and we had been raised by my mother and grandmother. My mother worked hard: she was a kindergarten teacher. I rewrote my childhood into a tough-luck tale, poor but livable. We had our fun. But recently I was visiting my sister Lisa, and as I held her new baby in my arms, she made a passing reference to our own childhood, and how I used to get whipped with a belt by my mother. I just stared at her.

"Belt?" I said, "I got whipped with a belt?" My sister's eyes widened. "Don't tell me you don't remember," Lisa said. "You don't remember The Belt?"

Of course. Of course I remembered The Belt. I did not remember it consciously, or even as an event in which I played a part, but I felt it as a twitch, an instinctive nod, a drop in my stomach. I felt the fear when Lisa said the words, I recognized something in her tone of voice. I knew that she'd said those same words to me years ago when we were kids, as a hushed warning, "Watch out, she's coming with The Belt." But this knowledge came on a gut level, subject to doubt and second-guessing, without an image-memory to substantiate it. Of the actual whippings I recalled nothing. Some careful editing had taken place. My memory of being whipped had been discarded, perhaps as contradictory to the childhood that I wanted to remember. I never wanted to see myself as the victim of violence, so I didn't. The whippings simply never happened. I had more acceptable memories that I returned to again and again, and I wore them smooth with constant mental polishing.

Can I trust my memory? I don't know. I had thought my mind was like a video camera, catching everything, but instead it has been more selective, crafting a self for me from select impressions. In the face of trauma, my memory's eye turned the lens away, or shut off the camera completely. I've memorized and rememorized other snippets of childhood, better moments—the five of us kids at Salisbury Beach in the winter, on the closed boardwalk, running from boarded-up shop to shop, with my mother and grandmother sitting a block away in the parked car, talking and sharing their thermos of coffee. I have created my own narrative around these preferred snapshots of memory. But I wonder about these other experiences, me with The Belt: Where have they gone? Has my knowledge of that event really been discarded, or is it just hidden? If I don't consciously accept those experiences as part of my history, do they still make up a part of who I am? Maybe they've woven themselves into my subconscious, they've helped to worsen my temper, or heighten my capacity for pain.

I wonder sometimes about the latent power of what I've turned away from. I wonder if ignoring those memories has defused their ability to hurt me, or if they lie in wait, an emotional land mine, waiting for my one false step that will spring them back up again, fresh and raw. I wonder how these discarded events have translated into my waking life. When I have my own children, will I reach for a belt automatically, without pause, without thinking or regret?

For years after my brother Michael's death, I did not think about him. If ever I came across something that triggered an association to him, my mind would click over to a mundane thought. Instead of Michael I would get a neat little reminder about the gas bill, the food in the fridge, the weather. I was automatic, a well-oiled little Forget Machine. My mind kept a wide distance from the latent tornado of emotion in my heart. And I thought this was a sign of progress. I had become a rational person, in control of my emotions. I was an adult. Sometime in the future, I told myself, I would look, I would bring Michael to the forefront of my memory. I would finally feel all the pain of our tangled relationship and recall the details of his young death, but in this distant future, my emotions would be quaint and controllable. Michael would be a safe story, a sweetly sad tale. From a distance of years, I would be able to love him.

Recently, I prepared myself to open those floodgates of memory. Thirteen years had passed since Michael's death, and I was ready for the maelstrom of grief, the onslaught of emotion. Enough time had passed. I had lived enough of my own life. But when I tried to summon up those memories of Michael, I found that they were no longer there. I pressed my memory for hard facts—Michael's exact eye color, the precise shade of his hair—and I came up blank. I couldn't remember the day he died, let alone the month or barely the season. I had only thin outlines, the same shadows of memory that had been there all along. After years of training my mind's eye away from Michael, I now found that I could no longer see him at all. Those memories had dissolved while my eyes were turned away.

These are the safe details, the ones I know: Michael was twenty-two when he died, and I was seventeen. He was still living at home. Michael was the only one of my brothers still living at home. In our three-bedroom apartment, the order of rooms was my mother's, Michael's, and mine. Around the time of his death Michael was not working, or his job was a meaningless one. I can't remember. I don't know what he did with his days. Maybe he was in school. I know that I was in high school, senior year, and applying to colleges. I know this fact because later, after they found his body, my college plans would all change when my mother blamed me for his death. *He wouldn't have done this*, she'd say to me at his funeral, *if you'd been a better sister to him*. And I would cancel my local college plans and move 3,000 miles away, clear out to California, just to get away from her and the power of that sentence.

But those physical details of Michael, where were those? How tall was he, what did he weigh? And then the circumstances of his death: How long had he gone missing? Who found his body? On what day of the week did he die? What was the weather like on that day, what was the name of the town they found him in, who was the police officer? What did his casket look like? Who came to the funeral? It's all a blank to me. Instead of being carefully packed away in my mind's cold storage, those facts had been surreptitiously moved out to the Dumpster.

I grew up in the Merrimack Valley, a cluster of towns in northeastern Massachusetts grouped around the once-booming textile mills on the Mer-

. . . .

rimack River. The *Lawrence Eagle-Tribune* was the only local newspaper in a twenty-mile radius, and everyone got it delivered. No one read the Boston newspapers so far north. The *Eagle-Tribune* still is the only local newspaper, and the chances are good that on any given Sunday, even now, I would recognize a face from the weddings page, or a family name from the obituaries. When I was growing up, the newspaper's small-town focus seemed myopic and claustrophobic, too limited in scope, but now I realize that the *Tribune*'s minute documentation of the Merrimack Valley is my only hope. Where my memory has failed, I now have a source to turn to.

The first articles appeared in the newspaper right after Michael had gone missing. I remember that the articles told too much—they revealed that Michael had epilepsy and asthma, that he needed daily medication to survive, that no one had seen him in days. As a teenager, I felt as if my life has been laid bare, my worst family secrets unearthed. Now it's that very unearthing that I need to see and learn from again, those secrets laid bare. I tell myself that time has healed me, and that now I am ready for an objective source, a brute listing of the facts. The newspaper, I tell myself, will know the truth.

As I drive through Lawrence now, it's a cold rainy autumn afternoon and the city looks like hell. Most of the buildings on downtown's main drag, Essex Street, are boarded up or shut down. The movie houses and department stores I remember being so impressed with are now rubble in vacant lots. The burger stand we used to love has been turned into a dingy Laundromat and the pharmacy where we bought our candy bars is now a storefront Puerto Rican church. Our old house on Tower Hill, once the best part of the city, has been subdivided into four ramshackle apartments with cheap raw-wood staircases tacked onto the sides of the house to meet fire-code regulations. The paint on the house is peeling and the windows of the upper floor are broken. Someone has placed an overflowing Dumpster right in the middle of the front yard, presumably to accommodate the refuse from the new apartments. Everything has changed, and it's hard to see even the bones of the familiar here. Lawrence is a slum. My mother is dying of cancer, and she calls Michael her "angel." We don't talk much. Nobody wants to bring up Michael anymore, nobody wants to rehash what really happened. If I want to remember, it's a journey I have to take alone.

The Lawrence Public Library keeps the daily editions of the *Eagle-Tribune* on microfiche dating back to the 1870s, and it's not hard to find spring of 1985, but the librarian looks at me with irritated disbelief when I tell her I'm not sure of the date I want to see. The rolls of microfiche come in two-week increments, she says, and if I don't know the exact date, then it's going to take me hours to find my brother's obituary. She says they have no index. I decide to start with the first thaw: March.

One of the first newspapers I scan through has a large photo on an inside page and I roll past it, then stop and turn back the knob to return the picture into the frame. It takes me a moment to realize that I'm staring at a picture of myself. I'm seventeen and sitting on a desk at North Andover High School, talking to a teacher, smiling. The picture is big. I had forgotten about this: a series of articles was published that spring on a group of us at the high school, six or seven students the reporter decided to dub "Seniors to Watch." In this article I am being solicited for my opinion about a teacher. I am quoted as saying that the teacher is fun to watch. It's a stupid thing to say, but then I am seventeen years old and prone to inanities. Something else I don't quite want to remember.

I scroll through more microfiche, week after week of town meetings and debates over pothole ordinances, and among the articles I am surprised to find a half dozen pictures of myself. In the photos, I have bleached blond spiky hair, too much jewelry, and I wear very mid-1980s new-wave clothing. The photos document me trying out for a play, singing in chorus, discussing college choices, opening my acceptance letters. By the end of April, it's clear that someone at the *Lawrence Eagle-Tribune* likes me.

That someone is a staff photographer. His name is Peter and he's thirty-two years old and we're dating. Every photo of me runs his credit at the bottom. He is my first real love and looking back, I am embarrassed by how obvious these photos are. I remember the relationship in its later years, when Peter and I fought over nothing and the difference in our ages pulled us apart, but in these pictures we are still infatuated with each other, and brazenly public in our display. Our relationship was absolutely taboo, and Peter was censured by his boss for it, once to the point of being fired. (A few days later he would be rehired after he threatened the newspaper with a lawsuit.) For my part, I was taken into the high-school-guidance counselor's office and lectured. None of it stopped us. We were determined to be together and just as determinedly, Peter chronicled the whole thing, shooting roll after roll of film of me, both for the newspaper articles and for himself. I never knew why he wanted so many photos of me. Now, thirteen years later, I understand. Looking through the lens of the Recordax machine, peering back through the newspaper photos and back through

. . . .

the lens of Peter's camera, I can see what he wanted to capture. That girl in the pictures is wholly, radiantly ignorant. She doesn't know about taxes, mortgage payments, deceit. She has no former lovers, no broken heart, no wizened cynicism. She is a clean slate, innocent and grinning and brimming with hope, and there's something spectacular about that, something you want to stare at, something worth capturing and fighting to keep frozen in time.

Despite the piles of contact sheets Peter would amass, he could not stop time, could not save me from the following month. As I continue to scroll through the microfiche, I notice a brief respite in my appearances in the pages of the *Tribune*, then my picture emerges again in late April as part of a McDonald's ad. I am posing for Peter, raising an Egg McMuffin to my mouth, pretending to be serious, with eight earrings in each ear and a pouf of bleached hair covering my eyes. My eyes show a gleam of arrogance. I have no idea that as the camera is shooting away, my brother is readying himself to die.

On Saturday, 4 May 1985, the first evidence of Michael's public life appears in the newspaper. On the front page, a single-column story is run alongside his 1981 high-school picture, with a headline reading, "Missing man needs daily medication." As I read the words now, I feel like the air has been kicked out of me. I turn my head away and take a breath. I tell myself that there is no door I can slam to keep this information at a distance: I want to read this, I need to read this. There is no punishment for reading this.

The lead line of the article begins ominously: "A North Andover man who needs medicine twice a day to prevent epileptic seizures has been missing for more than a week." Then I get my hard physical details, the very things I had most wanted to forget. Michael is described as being 5-foot-11, about 150 pounds. A slim build. Blue eyes, brown hair. I read the reporter's words with slow, deliberate concentration, as if the very act of reading them will recreate Michael in the flesh, there in the library. I believe for a moment that words have that kind of power.

I proceed slowly through the sentences. I let my eyes blur the words, turning the lines of the article into a shape, just column inches, about two by four, occupying only a small corner of the page. The information available to me is frustratingly finite. On this day in the Merrimack Valley, there are things more important than Michael's disappearance—there is room on this page for the Local Weather, including a Spore and Pollen Count; the Lotteries/Wingo numbers; an article celebrating Dennis "Oil

Can" Boyd's impeccable pitching for the Red Sox the night before. The author of Michael's first article—it has no byline—does not know the significance of what she's writing. She probably takes down reports like this from the police all the time. People sometimes go missing and later end up in Florida. In the cold spring, people need to see some sun, and they take drives. Especially bored young men with cars. People like Michael.

I focus again on the words. "He was wearing a blue jacket and white T-shirt," the article continues, "maroon pants and blue and white sneakers when last seen." Suddenly I remember Michael's blue jacket. It was a navy windbreaker with snaps. He wore it often. This is a fresh memory, untapped, not worn out with continuous use. This is crisp. I remember how the jacket hung on him, the water-repellent material it was made of, the white flannel lining. I remember his maroon pants, corduroys, Levi's, more rust-colored than maroon. He was thin, probably a 32-inch waist. He didn't eat much because of the medicine. This is what I was afraid of, what I'd been avoiding for thirteen years: the crispness of these memories. The closeness of the detail. I was afraid it would be like this, that when I would make myself look, I would see something that would give it all away. I will see that my mother was right, and that Michael's death was all my fault.

I remain seated at the Recordax machine and breathe. I tell myself the newspaper is only giving me facts, just facts that have been known for years, available here for anyone who cared to look.

My mother is interviewed for the article. "We were very close," she says to the reporter. "He would have told me if something was bothering him. . . . He had just bought a television and computer. . . . He was planning on going back to school." He had bought a computer? I don't remember that. And he was going back to school? Where? The University of Lowell? Northern Essex Community College?

My mother continues. "He can't have more than a week or two of medicine left," she says. "It must almost be gone. . . . He has to take it every twelve hours or he'll drop in place and go out cold."

When Michael first went missing, I didn't notice. For years I'd been trained to avert my eyes, so when he was gone his absence came as a relief. I could look freely around the apartment, at the walls, the sofa. I didn't have to creep past his bedroom door to get to the bathroom, I didn't have to keep my stereo down low. But then my mother became concerned. She hadn't heard from Michael in days. She called his friends, the same two or

· · · · · · · · ·

three guys he'd hung out with since high school—the fat kid, the stoner—
but no one had heard from him. The three of them had moved in the same
local circles, working crappy jobs night-shift, washing dishes at Denny's,
or working the booth at the self-serve gas station. They enrolled for a se-
mester here and there at community college up in Haverhill or Lowell,
then quickly dropped out. They were usually seen driving around town
together in their beat-up American cars, 1970s Chevys and Buicks and
Chryslers, getting high, smoking cigarettes and, killing time, maybe finding comfort in each other's lack of ambition. They stuck together. But this
time, however, nobody knew where Michael had gone.

There in the Lawrence Public Library, I sit close to the Recordax machine,
my shoulders hunched, the rolls of microfiche possessively piled up on my
lap. My muscles are tense. When the librarian walks close by, I arrange my
body so she can't see the screen. I am paranoid that someone will discover
who I am—recognize me from a picture?—as the uncaring sister of the deceased, and order me out of the library. I feel guilty, as if I am getting away
with something. My emotional flinch is Michael's detritus, his real legacy.
I try to relax. Maybe this time I realize that I won't be beaten for looking.

The second article appears on the next day, Sunday, 5 May, page two,
right underneath an AP wire piece on Reagan's trip to Bitburg. "Missing
man was seen Tuesday," is the headline, and the piece tells about how
Michael had been seen on the first of May when he took his girlfriend for
a two-hour ride in his car, a light green 1977 Buick Skylark with Massachusetts plates. The article doesn't state that the girlfriend was named
Michelle, and she was a little cross-eyed and she had a reputation. She was
fond of making out in the hallways of the high school. Michelle worked
menial jobs as Michael did, out on Route 114 in Lawrence. They dated for
a long time, probably three years, then broke up. She started seeing someone else. I don't know where he drove her that day. Maybe he wanted her
to go for a long drive with him, up into Vermont or New Hampshire.
Maybe he asked her to accompany him to Florida and she said no. Maybe
she talked about her new boyfriend, and how great he was. Maybe she
said she never loved him. The newspaper doesn't say.

On Tuesday, 7 May, the third and final article appeared, again on the front
page of the *Tribune*, running alongside that same high-school portrait of

Michael from 1981. The headline read, "Missing man found dead in Maine," and then the article followed.

> Michael Morrow, 22, of 68 Fernview Ave., was found lying on a mattress in a storage shed near an abandoned camp in Eagle Lake early Monday morning. . . . (Maine State Police Officer) Robinson said Mr. Morrow had apparently gone to sleep in the shed for the night, and died when temperatures dropped to 20 degrees. Eagle Lake is located 15 miles from the Canadian border—about a seven-hour drive from North Andover. Mr. Morrow had been dead about four days.

Four days. There in the Lawrence Public Library, sitting in front of the microfiche machine, I do the math. He saw Michelle on Tuesday, took her for a ride. They had been broken up for a few months, she had a new boyfriend, so they probably fought. He eventually dropped her off. He drove to Maine, seven hours. He ate at a McDonald's. He ran out of medicine. He went into the woods. He broke into a storage shed. He pulled a plastic tarp over himself for warmth, had a seizure, and passed out. There in the shed, he froze to death.

A shed, in the woods, in northern Maine, hours from the interstate, deep in the woods. Now I understand: Michael's goal was to get away from watchful eyes. He drove hundreds of miles away, out into the wilderness, to hide himself away in a shed where no one would be able to save him or even see him. Michael wanted to disappear completely, from our vision and from his own. His death was the ultimate act of self-erasure, after years of not being able to bear the sight of who he was, or even his reflection in my eyes. He wanted to step out of the picture, drop from sight. That last article in the newspaper doesn't even show a photo of that shed, that mattress, or that lake.

It's important for me to understand these facts. I feed quarters in the Recordax machine and make copies of each of the articles. I want to read them again and again, to understand the implications and tone of each word this reporter chose to write. I don't want to turn away from this information.

I spread the articles out on the adjoining desk and quickly draft up a calendar of the last week of April and first week of May of 1985. I circle dates. *Missing,* I write on 26 April. *Saw Michelle:* 30 April. *Died?* : 2 May, more or less, according to the police reports. 6 May: *Found.* Between the publication of the last two newspaper articles, between *Saw Michelle* and *Died?,* lies the information I'm really looking for. Michael made a deci-

. . . .

sion. On 1 May or thereabouts, something clicked in his mind. He began driving north. He knew he didn't have much medicine left, he knew he'd have a seizure. He knew he could die. Yet he drove on.

For those days after he went missing, I too am absent from the pages of the newspaper. There is no record of my oblivion, no excuse. I am not part of a McDonald's ad, a chorus concert, or some other banal high-school event. I am not a Senior to Watch. Perhaps I am hiding out in the Boston apartment of my thirty-two-year-old boyfriend, having my picture taken, myopically giddy with the attention I'm getting. Perhaps for the first time I'm realizing my power to be stared at, admired, adored. Perhaps I'm trying hard not to look back through the camera at Peter, trying not to see what I know, which is that there's something odd about our relationship, something unbalanced. Peter is, after all, nearly twice my age. He has had many girlfriends and even one marriage before.

Looking back, I see perhaps that what Peter wanted even more than a seventeen-year-old body was a seventeen-year-old mind, one without expectations or ego enough to make demands. He wanted to be seen as smart and worldly, and indeed that's how I saw him. I didn't question his ambition: the job of a local-newspaper photographer seemed very cosmopolitan to me. And of course, together as a couple, we enjoyed being a spectacle. We drew stares in the street and under-the-breath comments of strangers. If we ran across friends of mine in Boston, the scenario would always be the same. "Hey," they'd say, "this your dad?" and I'd laugh and Peter would turn away. "No," I'd say, and I wouldn't explain. I didn't think I needed to explain. I was moving through my life at breakneck speed, experiencing it all for the first time. I had no time to stop and think.

When my mother told me that the police found Michael's body, I know that I felt relief. I had just come in from a day at school and I remember where everyone was standing, my mother to my left, in the doorway of the kitchen, and my grandmother to my right, her head down. My mother just shook her head and said, "No," and I knew he was dead, that something terrible had happened, but instead of offering consolation, I went into Michael's bedroom, probably for the first time in my life, since he usually kept it locked, and I stole his albums. He had new-wave records I couldn't afford—Devo, Ultravox, the Tubes. I brought them back into my room and slipped them into my own collection. Maybe I was pretending that he'd lent them to me as an ordinary brother would, or maybe I needed to believe that we'd had that much in common, that music was the way we communicated from behind our walls. I know I didn't listen to those records once, nor have I since.

The last piece of Michael's public life appears in the newspaper on 7 May, on the obituaries page. The obituary itself is small, a rote listing of remaining family members and visiting hours at the funeral home, but most notably is the slug line below Michael's name—"Was an avid outdoorsman." An avid outdoorsman. This lie was obviously fed to the *Lawrence Eagle-Tribune* reporter by my mother, who thought a camping accident would be a noble death, or at least a more definitive one. Had Michael been an outdoorsman, or even a weekend camper, he would have known to pack a blanket, he would have known the importance of preparation. He would have known to bring his medicine, to let people know where he was headed. An avid outdoorsman doesn't break into a shed and pull a plastic tarp over himself for warmth.

After I leave the library, I drive across the city to the cemetery where Michael is buried. It's raining hard and the groundskeepers cease their work when they see me. They put down their tools and retreat under trees, and then watch as I walk down the rows of headstones, fruitlessly looking for his name. Perhaps this is cemetery protocol, something I was never aware of: don't let visitors see you dig.

After five or six rows, I see a familiar name and remember—because there was no money, Michael was buried in my grandmother's plot, under her last name. (My grandmother had bought her plot and headstone ten years before she died, and had her name and birthdate inscribed on it. For years the smooth stone awaited its final inscription. It would be finished in April of 1993, when my grandmother died of pneumonia.) Michael's name is now listed under hers on the back of the headstone, with all the inscriptions complete. I take my camera out from under my coat and focus on the name, and take a picture.

MICHAEL C. MORROW, 1963–1985

I turn my head and take a second picture, then a third, documenting the placement of this stone from each angle, then the trees, the fence. The rain opens up and I tuck my camera back under my coat and look around, trying hard to remember all of it, the white-gray sky and the smell of the rain and the freshly turned earth nearby. The groundskeepers get into the cab of their truck and wait me out. I think it rained the day of Michael's funeral. I try to recall anything about that day. Oddly, it occurs to me that Michael wore my shirt in his coffin. My mother had asked me on the morning of his wake, did I have a clean T-shirt for Michael, and I gave her one. I aim my camera down at the ground now and take a picture. I know in my heart that these photos will tell me nothing, will explain nothing of the past, but I want them anyway. If Peter the photographer were here with me, I would ask him too take a snapshot, up close and tight, to document something on my face, something that has changed, a layer of innocence lost: the realization that even when I did look, I was still not be able to see.

Dream, Memory, Story, and the Recovery of Narrative

by

KAREN BRENNAN

I want to begin with a dream I had last summer in Mexico. Because it was a dream with two parts to it, I entitled it: Dead Girl in Two Parts. What follows is a direct transcription from my journal. Part One: a girl in a school uniform falls from a ledge, from between the arches of a wrought-iron railing, to her death. I am sitting on the ledge and my daughter Rachel may have been there as well. The girl falls, I realize, because she is smaller than the arches and (I think at the time) the wind blows her off. She is simply swept through the railing. When I look down I see her little pile of school clothes—it seems to be all that's left of her. I feel regretful, but not horrified.

In the second part of this dream we—me, Rachel, and the little girl—are at the seashore, sitting on the beach, close to where the waves lap up. Suddenly a large wave washes over the little girl and kills her. Rachel and I look at her face staring up at us from beneath the water. It is a distinctive image, the face of the girl, eyes closed, under the shallow water that moves softly over her. I feel more than regret now; I feel guilt. I feel that one of us (Rachel) should have been more attentive. There is a sense that Rachel had been in charge of this girl. I am therefore a little annoyed with Rachel's irresponsibility, but this isn't a major annoyance. It's more like the resigned feeling I get in real life when someone's done something wrong (as if, for example, Rachel wrecks the car I give her) and I realize while it's futile to make a big deal over it, I am nonetheless pissed.

Approximately a month after I transcribed this dream in my journal I received a phone call in my Mexico flat at 6 A.M. informing me that my twenty-five-year-old daughter Rachel had been in a motorcycle accident

. . . .

and that she was currently in a deep coma in Denver General Hospital's intensive-care unit. Her friend, the driver was fine, but Rachel's CAT scan, the informant, a neurosurgeon told me, was very very ugly.

By 11 that morning I was on a first-class flight from León to Denver, sitting next to a woman who owned a travel agency in Guanajuato. She had been pretty, I remember, dark haired, dressed in cream-colored slacks and a white blouse. She wore a tiny silver watch on her wrist that, because I had misplaced my own somehow, I had recourse to consult now and again. She was on her way to Dallas for a romantic weekend with her husband. We had, what seems to me in retrospect, a pleasant conversation. I told her about Rachel's accident, she consoled me. I did not cry. I spoke reasonably, I thought at the time, having all the while that bizarre sensation that I was speaking someone else's words about someone else's daughter. I suppose I must have been in shock. I refused the first-class meal.

I remember that as we conversed my mind seemed to race along another track, somewhat at odds with our conversation. I imagined Rachel, even at that moment, woozily coming too, rubbing her eyes, her (perhaps) sore shoulders. I envisioned seeing her fully awake, out of the intensive-care unit by the time I would arrive, and I planned her homecoming, her few weeks of rest. I even went so far as to imagine my sudden memory of this time—on the first-class flight to Denver next to the woman in the cream-colored slacks, when I was terrified out of my mind. How amusing it would be in retrospect! How unfounded this terror, this unreasonable refusal of first-class food!

As it turned out, what was unfounded were these wishful thoughts. And in the months that have followed that August 18th day I have come to have a terrible familiarity with the way the mind—my mind—makes up comforting stories, this narrative propensity akin to the instinct for survival and just as precarious.

Rachel, in fact, continued in her coma for two months, more or less. I say more or less because, as it was explained to me, her injury was diffuse— literally, a diffuse axonal injury—and so her wake-up would be diffuse.

But when I arrived in Denver that first evening, I knew nothing of brain injuries, of axons, of intercranial pressures, of ventilation or tracheotomies, of motor strips, frontal lobes, aphasic disorders or unilateral neglects. I knew nothing of comas. What I knew was what I witnessed in the ICU unit, like a particularly grisly episode from *ER*: bodies being whirled by on stretchers, or corpse-like in beds, hooked up to monitors, a nurse with a clipboard positioned at the end of each.

Rachel was one of these bodies. She had a tube running down one nostril (nagogastric) for feeding, another in her mouth (intubation) for breathing. A little semicircle of her hair had been shaved, above the forehead on the left side, from which protruded a three-inch metal bolt. This was to measure her intercranial pressure. All the monitors flashed above the head of her bed on a large green screen: heart, respiration, blood oxygen, blood pressure, and intercranial pressure.

Rachel's eyes were closed. She had a small scrape on her cheek. The toes of her right foot were badly burned and grotesquely blistered. Occasionally she moved, but these movements were not reassuring; rather they were the unnatural movements of one who has severe brain damage called, in med-speak, posturing. At this stage, Rachel's postures were the most severe variety—decerebrate—indicating damage at a deep level of the cortex. They consisted of Rachel flexing her body and limbs rigidly into an extended position, her hands and feet turned inward in a bizarre way. Every time she postured, her intercranial pressures rose, meaning that the fluid in her brain was increasing to a dangerous level. Eventually another half-moon of hair would be shaved on the other side of her brow and a drainage tube inserted to draw off the excess fluid and blood.

But that evening, the evening I first saw her in her intensive-care cubicle with the tubes and drains and breathing steadily through the ventilator, her intercranial pressures were holding their own. I held her hand for a long while and then I went outside to smoke a cigarette.

Denver General Hospital is called, not so jokingly, The Gun & Knife Club. Some of its members—gangsters with cryptic faces and oversized jeans—smoked cigarettes nearby. In the orange lights I spotted and fixated on a little crop of dying zinnias. They seemed to be an important, if obvious, metaphor. Some had lost their petals, their color was drained in the artificial light. They were in concrete beds. A litter of cigarette butts surrounded their stalks. My thoughts were disorganized, I realized at the time—I had no story to tell myself, no future I could conceive of without horror. At which point a wheezing woman rolling an oxygen tank bummed a smoke from me. She was homeless, she explained, she had been evicted from her apartment. Now she was almost out of oxygen. I gave her a cigarette and twenty bucks. I sat in the grass.

My thoughts were disorganized and so I needed an idea. I recalled the Buddhist wisdom that impermanence is the true nature of things, the Hindu adage that everything is maya, illusion, that those who are enlightened can pass their hands through the fabric of the world. It was then that it occurred to me that Rachel would be OK. I had been looking at the sky, at a particular formation of gray clouds, and at the moon that was clear rimmed and precise—and it came to me. She'll be fine. It will go on and it will change and it will be fine. She will. I stubbed my cigarette and went back to the ICU unit. Around the bed next to hers, a group of doctors were "harvesting" a body—one of The Gun & Knife Club. The monitors were flat above the head of that bed, but Rachel's were beeping along— pulse 82, blood pressure 118 over 70, ICUs about 12. I held her hand. I kissed her. I began to talk to her as if she could hear, to call her back from wherever she was.

■ ■ ■

After the journal account of my dream of last summer, Dead Girl in Two Parts—I had appended a few notes. I noted that this was an important dream, one recalled with that special lucidity attributed to dreams of significance. I wondered about the two parts, the two scenes of the dream, wondered which came first in the actual dream and wondered why two parts. Were the two parts of my title, for example, a simple reference to the two parts of the dream or were they, in a Freudian ambiguity, literally two parts of the girl—physical or mental?

Accompanying my dream account and dream notes were a series of sketches. I sketched the arches of the railing through which the girl fell to her death, and I sketched the girl herself standing under an arch, a stick figure with a skirt. Then I sketched the relative positions of Rachel and myself on the ledge, behind the railing, looking down on the little pile of school clothes, which I also sketched. After my account of Part Two of my dream, I made only one sketch that I labeled "dead girl's face under a wave." The girl's eyes were closed, her hair snaked around her head, the wave replicated in a series of quivering lines, not unlike the surreal bars of some prison. Interesting, I noted, that in both dream scenes there was some reference to prison, both in the wrought-iron railing and in the lines I drew to suggest the wave over the dead girl's face. I wrote: Why a rooftop? Why a ledge? Why a threesome? Why two scenes? Why Rachel? Why guilty? Why pissed?

According to my notes, I had apparently figured that the dream had to do with me foisting off some little-girl part of myself, that I had been neglecting some self-care, that I was shirking some responsibility. But I was not satisfied with this glib reading—I had written "but the dream seems more complex than this."

Coming upon this account of my dream after Rachel's accident, of course I read it in a new light. Now the dream seemed, absolutely, to be a portent of some sort. Indeed the sketch of the dead girl's face under the wave struck me as bearing an uncanny resemblance to Rachel's face in her coma, a coma that lasted, by the way, for a grueling two months. And weren't the lines of water moving across her face, in fact, a brilliant figure for the hazy boundary that separated us at this time, she in her world, me in mine? Such an interpretation defied all that was reasonable and yet, oddly, was the most "reasonable" of any I could come up with: that is to say, it was able to connect most of the disparate elements into something that cohered. On the other hand, it was an entirely "unreasonable" account. What Aristotle would call the probable impossible, more the material of fiction than "reality."

For in Freud's schematics of dream interpretation, doesn't the dreamer participate in the dream interpretation precisely to discover the latent content of her unconscious? Certainly, a portent would refute all that. The significance of a portent exists outside the dreamer, in both space and time. A portent conflates time and space, conflates, in Yeats's formulation, the dreamer and the dreamed.

Still, as I sat at Rachel's bedside, looking at her perhaps dreaming face, the monitors measuring the steady waves of her vital functions, I recalled my dream of the dead girl in two parts and wondered which part was me and which part Rachel.

Since that first evening I continued to speak to her as if she could hear me. I told her her life's story over and over. What I couldn't remember, I invented. I felt that it was more important to deliver a coherent narrative than to be faithful to a disjunctive truth. Even though I value fragmentation in all its forms, I felt that had I been lying there in some kind of netherworld, I would want a story that made sense, whose points A and B and C were nicely connected.

But whose story was it? I became, more than occasionally, confused. Parts of my own life mingled weirdly with my story of hers just as, during that time, the outside world seemed to take on the sensual attributes of this inside, hospital one. I spent, on the average, eight hours a day by—or more usually in—her bed, and so I suppose it was reasonable that during my infrequent ventures to that otherworld espresso machines would sound like the suctioning apparatus for her trach, that someone's beeper would send a rush of alarm through me.

Finally, she began to really awaken, her left eye cracked open to reveal a tiny, beautiful chink of blue iris now roving back and forth, to sounds, to

· · · · · · · · ·

light; and she began to move her left thumb over the knuckles of my hand in an actual caress, a response; and on one joyous afternoon, she reached and pushed a strand of my hair behind my ear, taking the initiative (a higher brain function) in an activity that I had neglected as a matter of course. Finally and suddenly, when all these things and more happened with a rapidity that stunned me, having become accustomed to the tabula rasa of her sleeping, motionless face, and our merging, far from loosening, seemed to intensify, at least in the mind of this dreamer. At home, in front of my medicine-cabinet mirror, for example, my hand through my hair felt oddly like her hand; and in my own bed before sleep, I felt my body assuming her positions, right arm locked upward against my cheek, fingers rigid and clenched.

And when she began to speak—her first sentence on 15 November was, gratifyingly, "I want my mom"—you'd think that hearing her voice would deliver me to myself, but it didn't. She spoke in breathy whispers at first, and so did I. We spoke endearments and bodily discomforts, having to pee and having to move the covers over our shoulders. Around this time I felt light-headed as I walked through the hospital corridors; it seemed to me the ground was shifting under my feet. Rachel's head lolled to one side; at that point she was unable to hold it erect.

■ ■ ■

I might say: I love my mama. She is the one. Next to her everyone pales. That's the truth of it. But I'm too old for these feelings. I tell her this. She says, Oh who cares? Or I think she does. She is wearing a green sweater covered with white vines that are of the same fabric of the sweater, which is wool. In the rectangle of the door, which is blue and rough, there is a toilet. There is a white towel on a floor of many small tiles of many hues of blue. The grouting is not clean. She is standing in her bare feet in front of the medicine-cabinet mirror and it is a sorrow to me that I cannot see her reflection, only her right-side-up face, which is to me quite beautiful. She says, Oh I'm a vain old woman. Vain perhaps, Mama, I say.

Sometimes she asks, How are you doing? How are you doing, Lou? Are you feeling good? I say, Totally good, Madre. I call her all names for mother or that is as many as I can get a hold of. I remember words, this is true, language is my strongest point.

Matcha, I say, Why does everyone have to watch me pee? No one does, she says, see? I'm not watching. I'm brushing my teeth, I'm watching the brushing of my teeth. It's OK, Matcha, I say, you can watch me pee. You can give me a shower. You can snuggle with me at night when we hear the floor creak and someone who may be opening the door, only you say no.

■ ■ ■

As of this writing Rachel, after five and a half months of hospitalization, has been home for two months. Her language is completely intact; indeed it is eloquent. Her sense of humor is as sharp as ever. She is attentive; she is perceptive; she is occasionally philosophical and frequently wise. Her most severe deficit—aside from some paralysis that affects the right side of her body and keeps her confined, for the moment, to a wheelchair—is her short-term memory. Although memory deficit is common in traumatic brain injuries (TBIs), Rachel's seems especially severe. There have been some small improvements, but she frequently cannot remember from one five-minute segment to the next. If, for example, I ask her fifteen minutes after dinner what she ate, she'll shrug and say in her wry fashion, "Who can remember?" She's aware that her memory sucks but who knows how to cure it?

■ ■ ■

14 March 1996: "Dear Sweet Diary: I feel as though I'm waking up from a bad dream because I mean I don't know the difference between right or left. I mean I do, but I'm trying to simplify everything. Today I have been learning about myself. That is to say I'm learning about the details of my accident. So granted I may never ever walk again. My memory sucks. But I'm beginning to understand what happened to me and such. Except I have very little to do with, well what will I do in the future? Perhaps I will become a famous shoe tyer. But maybe not, maybe I will be quite ambitious. Maybe I will become a teacher like my madre. So I hope I'm well enough to conquer the world again."

■ ■ ■

Memory, according to Henri Bergson, occupies the space between mind and body. It conveys mind to body and body to mind. It gives us our qual-

. . . .

ity of life—makes possible, in other words, the narratives that keep our lives going forward to the next thing. If the thing is not *next* it loses its richness—isolated and unlinked to a history, it becomes meaningless, even ridiculous. Biologically and neurologically we are creatures of context, of narrative.

Consider, for example, the activity of the neurons or brain cells. Unlike the body's cells that divide and multiply, microcosmically illustrating the propagation of the species, neurons are systems of communication. Their most salient features are a clutch of dendrites that branch out to receive information across the synapses between cells and a single, long axon that reaches to the synapse—literally the space between neurons—through which chemical and electrical information are conveyed to the next cell.

By nature, then, the activity of the neuron is narrative, metonymic, associative. The information conveyed by each neuron accumulates along a complex circuitry of neurons and produces a thought, a corresponding action in the mind-body. If the information that passes from neuron to neuron is somehow tampered with—if the transmitters or receptors are artificially altered by drugs or disease, for example—memory, at its very biological foundation, will be altered or even incapacitated.

■ ■ ■

Her feet are covered with blue veins. Blue veins on a blue tiled floor. So many blues. Which kind of vein are you? I ask her. She is brushing her hair, which is brown; which flies up into the brush like TV static.

I keep having the same dream. I do not remember details. Try to remember, she says. Was there a wave? Was there wind? I think, I say. Was there a girl? Perhaps, I say. Everything is skewed a little to the left: the table, the chair with its black-and-white pictures of parasols and ladies, the overhead fan with its wide white wings. All to the left. Where am I? I say.

You are here, she says. She leans over and puts her mouth to my ear. Here. Her breath is hot, like a mirror glare. Like a glint on tin. I say, If not *her*, then what? and this makes me worry. But she says, Don't worry, just enjoy everything for the time being. Just look at that little fly on the kitchen table having a sip of orange juice or listen to the car roll by outside or brush your hair, here Lou, brush your hair.

. . . .

She both understands everything and doesn't understand a thing. She goes on as if all were normal. She hands me the brush. Then she puts on lipstick. Next she will put lipstick on me. Why would I want lipstick? I am thinking, but I love my mama.

■ ■ ■

Memory is always configured on a gap—to re-member suggests the forgetfulness, the loss upon which it is founded. This forgetfulness, too, has its biological equivalents in the neurological activity of the brain. Indeed in this most complicated of operations, the electrical impulses received by each neuron are converted to chemicals—packets of neurotransmitters—which are able to diffuse across the synaptic gap and activate the electrical signal in the next neuron. The process of conversion itself, as well as the infinite number of variables in each neuron, point to what has vanished as well as to what can be retrieved, point to the loss of the Real (in the absolute, psychoanalytic sense) and the construction of a representation.

Narrative has been the business of my life for many years now, both as a teacher and writer of fiction, but it was not until Rachel's brain injury that I realized these biological correlatives. We are hardwired into narrative; it is, I would go so far to say, the purpose and not merely the effect of memory. The account of my dream of the dead girl, for example, is presumably based on my memory of it—but this memory is, at best, a shaky representation of a neurochemical process whose sparks and ebbings are irretrievable (if not nonsensical). What is important, we've learned from Freud, is the representation itself, assembled from whatever fragments, into a story that is the very material that divulges, if we are attentive, unconscious wishes.

Even our interpretation of dreams reveals a wish to make sense of the fragmentary, to weave into story, into history, an event which, unconnected to the life, may be troubling. Why else would I suspend my disbelief in portents but that I yearn for narrative continuity, even in retrospect, something to explain, however mystically, the strange and terrible turn of my daughter's and my life. The narrative inclination takes precedent, in this example, over reason itself, over what we know to be sensible and "true" about human experience. Which inclines me to believe that these fictions we call narrative and memory are at the foundation of our beings.

■ ■ ■

The days are a daze. I like that sentence because it is so truthful. I say it's the one true thing I am feeling. This feeling which is the urge to push away some part of the air from in front of my face. It would be risky, I know. Because behind that part of air, there are things I actually want to forget. Now that I've said it and the minute I say it I think, no that's not true. Because why? Because it isn't.

Most of the time I just float in. I laugh quite a bit. Things strike me funny and I can feel my lips go way up over my teeth in a manner that is not very attractive. The photo of my great-grandfather hanging on the wall in a brown frame is really quite funny to me, for example, although I couldn't tell you why exactly. He is very faded and maybe it's the fadedness of him that is so like my own idea of things these days. That we all exist in a vault. That inside the vault are scraps with no meaning—torn photographs, letters from people we don't know, receipts, single words, like jewelry.

■ ■ ■

You ARE my memory, Rachel tells me, and it's true. I remember the actual as well as I can and what I don't remember, I shamelessly invent. You got up, you brushed your teeth, your therapists came over, and you stood up; you walked with your walker; you made everyone laugh when you asked for a big-assed cup of coffee. You admired my outfit and said, "You've got it going on, girlfriend."

What will we do tomorrow? she worries. She has less tolerance for the uncertainty of the future than the rest of us. What do I have to do? she says. We make lists of questions and answers; we record her voice and her day's activities as they occur into a palm-sized device called a voice organizer; we plan. We talk. Together we assemble an imperfect representation, a narrative we can rely on nonetheless, one which compels us forward to the next thing.

In brain-injury literature there are several pathological behaviors associated with short-term memory loss and these behaviors, I was stunned to discover, correspond to narrative pitfalls and graces, that is to say, to the way in which we all make narrative texts. Perseveration is the inclination of the brain-injured patient to get stuck, obsessively on one track and to thus repeat over and over this one-tracked concern.

Perseveration—a word I find especially illuminating, to persevere too much, as I take it—reflects a rigidity on the part of the perseverator. A failure of imagination, a failure of metonymy, of association, free or otherwise. The perseverator can only repeat, sometimes in different words—Rachel, for example, is quite eloquent in her perseverations—and this repetition while in some cases may reinforce a narrative cannot of itself deliver a narrative. The perseverator suffers from too much focus and a surfeit of schemes. It is the student of writing who can't seem to move beyond his one good idea, the student of fiction who gets stuck in a scene with a character who doesn't move or change. We all know these authors, these dull and doomed texts.

And while perseveration is this rigidity, this refusal or inability to change tracks, confabulation is exactly the opposite. To confabulate—literally to replace fact with fantasy in memory—is to wildly trope. The confabulator suffers from an unruly, unstoppable imagination, an inability to focus and develop a theme. The brain-injured confabulator concocts wild tales to compensate for his lack of memory—he fills in the gaps. Back when Rachel was confabulating, she thrilled (as well as alarmed) me with her imaginative richness that seemed, for all its craziness, to be odd and accurate tropes for her situation. Cinderella smashed all the windows, she announced one day, sadly. On another occasion she confided that she *knew* we were on a plane over Vietnam and that she had been shot. Then there was time, during a particularly arduous session of stretching her spastic arm, when she joyfully proclaimed to her occupational therapist that she was giving birth to a baby. The confabulator is compelled by the absence of specific space/time representations. There is no focus to her story, no organizing principle, and, perhaps in extreme cases, a failure of mimesis.

Having made these links to all-too-common narrative pathologies, it occurs to me that without the compulsive activities of confabulation and perserveration a written narrative (much less a fiction) of any interest at all could not be made. The memoir I am at such pains to deliver, woven among bits of speculation not unrelated to my situation and your situation, perseverates in its relentless return to several subjects, not to say several perseverating rhetorical strategies. I suppose I confabulated. Had there really been decaying zinnias in a concrete bed in the Denver General smoking area? Had the moon really been as I described it, clear rimmed and precise? And my companion on Flight 331 from León, Mexico to Denver, Colorado, had she actually worn cream-colored slacks and not,

. . . .

say, a brown twill skirt? Had it been, in fact, Flight 331? Or have I forgotten in the blur of anxiety and sorrow the details of my own experience? I confabulate to fill in the gaps. I perseverate to bide time. Both activities rely on, are compelled by my forgetfulness; indeed my narrative, I believe, benefits from this forgetfulness. I believe it brings me mysteriously closer to the truth.

■ ■ ■

I think I am going somewhere. I think I must have been in an accident. I was not driving. I do not remember it.

There was a piece of light that evaded me then I was doomed.

She wears red lipstick, as do I.

When I woke up I was in a cloud, so really I have not woken up. You could say that. On the other hand, a building has a reality and so does a banana. All things exist therefore I do.

Only I am looking at her string of pearls. Very pearly white. I finger them with my fingers and blow a bubble into my milk. Outside the world is covered up and cold.

■ ■ ■

Yet there is something in us—in me—that yearns for the seamless life, for a resolution (termination? thanatos?) of the chaotic or unbearable. Conventionally speaking, a memoir promises to deliver the kind of product that will pacify my anxieties. In its seamlessness—its artful seamlessness, I should say—the memoir seeks to fulfill a certain kind of desire for narrative "truth." It is nothing, I realize nervously, if not credible. Because a fiction is not concerned with credibility in the same way, it's able to represent the disjunctiveness of what's real. Stylistically, it can indulge and even parody its own compulsive operations. Consider this perseverative bit from Donald Barthelme's "The Falling Dog": "A dog jumped on me out of a high window. I think it was the third floor, or the fourth floor. Or the third floor." Or this confabulation from *Ulysses*: "Walk on roseleaves. Imagine trying to eat tripe and cowheel. Where was that chap I saw in that picture somewhere? Ah, in the dead sea, floating on his back, reading a book with a parasol open."

The perseverations and confabulations of Barthelme and Joyce—and every other writer we cherish—constitute what we value of their style. To rethink style in terms of compulsive pathological brain operations might recall Jacobsen's famous study of aphasics and the links to metaphor and metonymy he discovered in their flawed speech patterns. His point, like mine, is that these patterns persist in nonpathological brain states as effects of compulsive organic activities. Any good writer knows this, which is why we speak so lovingly of indulging our obsessions, of making use of our compulsions to confabulate and/or perseverate. There is no normal narrativemaking.

At some point I hit upon the idea that what I could do for Rachel that her therapists could not do, perhaps, as feelingly, is offer her help with storymaking, with narrative. She has always been a talented storyteller and her language abilities and imagination have endured despite severe brain trauma. So I've become her writing teacher. Tell me a story, Rachel, I urge. Make something up. At first her stories were nonnarrative confabulations. There is Justine with a bee on her head. What about Justine? I prompted. What about the bee? Rachel smiled, shrugged. That's it, she said. That's all. The end. Eventually the stories would acquire a narrative feel, but the narratives would be flat. Once upon a time, she might begin, but then the character, Justine, or a small, pale, weak girl, or whoever, would simply drift into some arena—the desert, the city, the mall—and stay there. These stories were shapeless, lacking destinies. Still a sense of conflict was beginning; built into the notion of small, pale, and weak is the trajectory of its plot. Lately her stories attempt some kind of resolution: a very small weak girl struck out for the desert because she had been left alone and her father and mother had died and there was nothing she could think of to do but to go to the desert and weep under a mesquite. On the way there, however, she met a nice friend who happened to be called Charles. He had a bunch of chocolates with him, which he shared with the small, weak girl and which revitalized her. They had a great time and eventually they went to Las Vegas. The end.

A sense, however tentative, of one idea proceeding from another, of a beginning and an ending, is not only indicative of Rachel's recovering memory but, it seems to me, is crucial in generating her memory along its circuitry of synapses. Narrative is the practice of memory and forgetfulness; it is how we accumulate experience and develop imaginative skills.

. . . .

Our stylistic compulsions make us utterly individual or, to put it another way, our individuality is generated by our style. Which is to say the infinite variety of our neurons—we each have about 200 billion—ensures our stylish individualities.

Having said all this, I confess that I'm working hard to keep this account from flying in all directions. Because these days I live in terror of the fragmentary—those blown-apart bits and pieces. I'm eschewing the loose end, the ragged transition, the unresolved thought—but like every *unheimlich* they are poking through to haunt me. Just as in my life these days I am trying to keep everything together—Rachel, the five or six therapists who've become part of our weekdays, my students, my job, this piece of writing—and I sense from time to time a little tearing at the seams. I ignore those scratchy sounds. I proceed as if all will resolve itself. This is my assumption, my faith. In the space of a phone call my life went from a kind of random self-indulgence—I was melancholic, moody, bored—to a passionate necessary-ness. But I don't know the ending to this story, which is why the experience of writing it is so unsettling. I imagine the best because it's my only choice—it's the way I want to live.

Still my head buzzes unpleasantly. There are worries. There are undecided questions and shaky transitions and thoughts right now that I have trouble completing. I'd like you to know that I'm writing this in my basement under these bare bulbs that hurt my eyes and that it's snowing outside and that I can hear the creak of Rachel's wheelchair overhead—she's put on rap again—and that I just quit smoking. I want to say this is not a memoir (too messy) and not a theory (too untheoretical) and not a fiction (too true); and that it occurs to me that the buzzing in my head is due to radon, probably, and that it's cold in the basement and I detest snow and that like Rachel I ask why why why? Why me?

Because it's unbelievable, isn't it, when life suddenly assumes the grotesque and overblown proportions of dreams? But which is the construction, the dream or the life? It occurs to me that we approach our dreams like "fiction," like impossibilities, that we've divided dream from life in order to preserve the smooth, untroubled narrative of our dailiness. Rachel, for example, frequently feels that she's in a dream or is waking from a dream. She asks: Is this reality? And I think that her reality is literally unbelievable to her—she cannot conceive of it.

■ ■ ■

I say one thing, then another. I say her skirt is unfathomably beautiful. I say the wind will tear at her hairnet. I say look closely, that's me feeding the fish. Leaning over and seeing my face superimposed on the faces of the fish.

Here is my red jacket with the purple trim, my fake leopard hat, my woolen scarf, my mittens.

Here is my bad arm which I put in first, then my good arm. Here are my feet, which no longer move.

Here is Matcha, my dear mother, hanging our clothes on the line and here I am on a roof looking down. No wonder I feel off-balance. Such beautiful laundry! I yell. What? she says. You're not making sense.

Then she throws me something. It is a red item with a hook. A bra? I say. Something to eat?

■ ■ ■

Recent brain-mind theory suggests that there is no division between the brain and the mind, between, that is, biology and what we call consciousness. What this means is that there are no qualitative boundaries separating dreaming and waking, in this paradigm, just a few chemical change-ups.

The new, hypertextual theories of dreams sound oddly like postmodern theories of literature. Dreams are no longer vehicles to texts of some occluded unconscious, but are themselves, postmodernly, their own writerly pastiches of significance. Harvard psychiatrist Allen Hobson calls them "virtual representations" and "the fictions we live by." If there are purposes for dreams, argues Hobson, it is that the souped-up programs of REM sleep reinforce memories and rehearse plans of action, embedding these plans and memories in rich systems of neurocircuitry, which we could call meaning or even life. Our dreams are our testing grounds; we try new things, we readjust, we plan. They are the field upon which we invent the life.

No two brains are alike. For this reason, brain theory has it that no two traumatic brain injuries are alike. But despite the heartening open-endedness of this fact, the medical profession in its practice cleaves to its old self-protective generalizations—"She may never wake up,"—false—"She

.   .   .   .

seems acutely aphasic"—false—"She will never be able to lead an independent life"—don't know.

What I have found is that just as all good narratives defy teleological, economical, linear models in favor of messy, subversive, nonlinear ones, recoveries from brain injuries create their own disordered stories. Boundaries, such as those between fact and fiction, dreams and reality, and even, in our case, mother and daughter, are dissolved in order to make a place for something new, rich, and surprising to occur. This new "something" is identity—whatever transitory fiction we call self—and the project is not so different from what I, as a feminist lit crit/ creative writer, have been doing for the past ten years—dissolving/subverting/transgressing gender and genre boundaries in order to assemble new subjectivites.

Which brings me back (or forth) to my dream of the dead girl in two parts, the overdetermined feature of my own messy narrative. What does the dream mean for my life? What am I meant to draw from those strangely prophetic scenes of me and Rachel looking, in two ways, at a girl who died, tragically and almost, now that I think of it, comically? One minute a ledge. Then a fall. One minute a beach. Then a wave. A rehearsal, I think, for what will come inevitably in any life and from what perspectives we are able to witness. From above, looking down at that little pile of school clothes or at eye level as the wave comes even before we knew it came, that quickly. And suddenly as I write this down I know what that dream is about, and how I am bound to be in those two places—the ledge and the shore—even as this writing seeks to conflate and distinguish the memoir from the theory from the fiction and especially as I struggle to reimagine my daughter and myself.

■ ■ ■

The sun is melting the snow between my madre and me. When I touch her hair I can feel the feel of my hands running through. Who are you, Madre? I say. Are you on the inside or the outside, because honestly, I can't tell.

"El Camino Real"

. . . .

by
JAMES A. MCPHERSON

I

Each day, from early morning until the evening hours, at the exit of the Town and Country Mall on El Camino Real in affluent Palo Alto, California, a middle-aged white man in a weathered gray down jacket and a brown touring cap stands, looking downward, always downward, while holding a cardboard sign. The sign reads: "I am a Christian man." This man is a professional beggar. Begging, it seems, has become his job, and he has established a prescriptive easement, if not a spiritual fee simple, in his space just at the exit of the affluent mall. The security guards never chase him away. Whenever someone, driving away from that consortium of up-scale shops, stops and hands money to him, the solitary man becomes animated. He smiles, showing decayed teeth, and looks intently at the face beyond the hand reaching out of the car window. He smiles with the glow of communal connection. He says, always: "God Bless you."

This broad commercial roadway, El Camino Real (or Route 82), runs northward as far as San Francisco and as far southward, I have been told, through a great number of identical but differently incorporated communities, as Los Angeles and the Pacific Coast. The Spanish conquistadors who first cut this highway named it "The Royal Road." It was aptly named. The rising affluence of this area of northern California, buoyed by the Silicon Valley to the south, has accelerated the number of standardized malls in each of the small communities along this road: Blockbuster Videos, Safeway stores, Carl's Jrs., Banks of America, Starbuck Coffees.

. . . .

Even the ethnic restaurants—Chinese, Spanish, Japanese, Korean, Ethiopian, Indian, Caribbean, Greek, Italian—are standardized in their sad lack of exoticism. This is so because there are just too many of them on each block. Within the banks and commercial outlets, clerks and salespersons—Hindu, Ethiopian, Spanish, Korean, Chinese, Southeast Asians, and, yes, even black and white—testify by their presence that a demographic revolution has already taken place here, has already been standardized in commercial terms. Each morning, all along El Camino Real, there are groups of Spanish men, clustered on both sides of the highway, waiting to be picked up for day-labor. And, of course, there are the homeless people, some riding bicycles, some pushing shopping carts loaded with their material possessions, peddling and pushing, clothed in a pathetic individualism, among the cars and human traffic. The tragic arch of this highway grows out of the fact that the high-tech munificence of San Jose and the Silicon Valley and the human muscle of the barrios are locked in an extremely unfair competition. Two radically different worlds, or economic worldviews, are in contention here, and there is really no doubt which world will lose. But still, the descendants of the Conquistadors and the root-races native to this region, stand, defiantly, each morning, waiting to connect with work.

Last September, when I first observed the man at the Town and Country Mall, I gave money to him. I promised myself, then, that I would always stop and give money to such people. I made an easy moral-dandy judgment that it was *shameful* that the State of California, sitting on the ninth largest economy in the world, could not do more to help such people. I promised myself that I would remain an outsider to this casual indifference, and maintain my own moral integrity, only as long as I continued to give money to beggars. But after several months I slowly began to end this practice. There were just too many people—black, white, male, female—begging at stoplights and at street corners up and down that road. To my own credit, I will add that this withdrawal of moral effort and energy was a gradual and unconscious process. The efficiency of my daily commutes up and down that road required that I conform to the flow of traffic. The average speed on El Camino is 35 to 50 miles per hour. Beyond this, I live in a townhouse inside a gated community of townhouses, one with its own private road. People inside the gate love the private road (for residents and their guests), the elegant swimming pool, the sauna, the clubhouse, our own Spanish maintenance men, as well as the privacy and the quiet. When I turn my car right, off the busy El Camino

Real, onto our private road, I abruptly enter into another world, an *inside* one, a gated one. This is a world in which the other holders of fee simple are hardly ever seen; a world in which the Spanish maintenance men are always busy watering plots of grass or vacuuming fallen leaves. But, slowly and much more consciously than I would like to think, these men, *inside* the gate, have become, like the groups of Spanish men along El Camino Real, and like the middle-aged white man standing by the exit of the Town and Country Mall, no more than abstractions. I had accepted them as only part of the landscape.

Then, several months ago, one rainy afternoon, the flow of *outside* human traffic intruded into this haven. A knock on my door, something that had grown unfamiliar to me, brought me back to consciousness. The uninvited visitor was a middle-aged, overweight white female, one dressed almost in rags. She had already begun to run away when I opened the door. "I'm hungry," she explained. "I was knocking on doors asking for money for food." I speculated that she was just as surprised to see me, a black male in such an affluent context, as I was to see her. I know I was surprised, if not shaken, to see a person looking like her *inside* our gated community. I reached into my pockets for some change, and it was then that I remembered the pledge I had made to myself back in the early fall. I located my wallet and gave her ten dollars, most of it for the man outside the Town and Country Mall, whom I had begun to ignore. I realized, after this encounter, that both of them must have had stories to tell and that I, as a writer, should have been interested in imagining the failures or the tragedies or the betrayals, or even the comic confidencings, that had led both of them, two white people within a mostly white community of great affluence, to go begging. But something had grown dull, or coarse, *inside of me*, and had prevented me from placing value on their stories. I realized, then, that the gated community in which I live and make my reality had taken up an existence inside of me.

Since that rainy winter day I have kept careful watch for the middle-aged white beggar at the exit to the Town and Country Mall. I have looked for him each time I go into the mall or drive past it. Why does he always stand at the exit and not at the entrance? It would seem that more people would be taking extra money into the mall than out of it. Why does he wear the same costume day after day? Why does he seem to stand at perpetual attention? Why does he choose to stand in the rain? What does he do with the money? Most important of all, I have tried to imagine the essentials of his story. If I can avoid being cynical and dismissing him as

. . . .

just another hustler who, like a great number of people in California, have made a lucrative profession out of begging, and if I can employ the full powers of my imagination, I can see coming into focus something brilliantly simple in its complexity. I can see a story: this man, who is only masquerading as a beggar, is in reality a philosopher and a teacher. His real job is to remind the affluent shoppers, only when they *leave* the Town and Country Mall, of their moral obligations to all the other beggars to the north and south along El Camino Real. The philosopher wearing a worn down jacket is really conducting a semisecular *church* at the exit of the Town and Country Mall.

Consider the existential undercurrents of his sermon:

The written words on his cardboard sign proclaim to the outside world: "I am a Christian man." And his oral response to any gesture of human kindness ("God bless you") are in perfect balance. The two taken together, the flowing between the outside and what is inside, recall to mind the expression, "Let the words of my mouth and the meditation of my heart be acceptable in thy sight." Inside his disguise, this philosopher is quietly announcing a solution to one of the most fundamental problems in the Western tradition—the proper relation between the outer and the inner, the outside and inside of the self. He is suggesting a principle of alternation. Also, perhaps, he is offering insights into the reasons for the rise of the autobiographical forms of writing—the memoir and the personal essay—that has engendered distaste, if not contempt, among the watchdogs of the cultural establishment. Such clues to the importance of the relation of what is inside the self to what is outside the self may well reside in many such refugees from middle-class society. This beggar/philosopher, then, is only reminding the affluent shoppers, *even if they do not stop to give to him*, to remember his message and to act kindly toward the other beggars *outside* the Town and Country Mall, along The Royal Road.

II

It was Saint Augustine who advised that "memory is the belly of the soul." This is the place which, in recent years, had begun to challenge the supremacy of the novel form as the finest portrait of the culture. There is an increasing inwardness in narrative expressions, whether in memoirs or in autobiographical essays. The university at which I teach, the University of Iowa, now has two nationally noted writing programs: the Writers' Workshop, and a new Non-Fiction Writing Workshop. As many students flock to get into the former as into the latter. And each summer, the university sponsors Summer Writing Institutes for elderly people, who come from all parts of the country to spend two to six weeks committing their memories to paper. Even in this gated community, with its quiet and its remove from the flow of life along El Camino Real, there is an inward turn. Each Thursday afternoon, at 3:00 P.M., a group of the residents meet to share with one another the contents of their memories. One elderly man, a former officer in the O.S.S., is writing an autobiographical novel about his exploits in France and in North Africa. Another elderly woman, from Texas, is recapturing her family-centered youth in a small Texas town. Another woman, from Kansas City, is reconstructing the texture of the Midwest out of which Harry Truman and Kansas City jazz came. And still another woman, crippled since birth, and childless, is fingering the wounds left by her childhood. There is a growing inwardness in most of our expressions. But whether this withdrawal has been caused by the bent toward a thin entertainment culture in the world outside our own, or whether it is a retreat from the fragmentation and uncertainty of the larger world, has yet to be decided. Whatever the cause, this turning inward, beyond its narcissism, may be the expression of a private yet communal effort to relocate some human essentials that have been obscured, if not lost altogether.

It was the Greek philosopher Plato whose teaching about eternal forms, or ideas, laid the basis in the Western tradition for the division between the inner and the outer. His idea of the human soul as akin to the "intelligible" world but having fallen into the "sensible" world is the first barricade between the inside and the outside. Plotinus later built on Plato's "Allegory of the Cave" by connecting the intelligible, inside world with the Divine Mind. When the soul looks inward, according to Plotinus, it sees a Divine Mind and an inner world that is radically different from the sensible world. Augustine took up this same problem in the tenth book of his *Confessions*. Because he was laying the theological foundations for the Western Catholic Church, Augustine modified his old doctrine of predestination—the doctrine spelled out in his earlier *On Grace and Free Will*, that God has an eternal plan to give grace to some people and not to others—and posits that Plato's idea of the "fall" is in reality original sin in the sense suggested in the Book of Genesis. The inner world, then— memory—is like the courtyard of an inner palace, open at the roof, from which the soul looks up to God.

· · · · · · · · ·

Augustine writes:

You are always there above me, and I rise toward you in my mind. I shall go beyond even this force which is in me, this force which we call memory, longing to reach out to you by the only possible means and to cling to you in the only way it is possible to cling to you. . . . So I must go beyond memory, too, if I am to reach the God who made me different from the beasts that walk on the earth and wiser than the birds that fly in the air. I must pass *beyond memory* [my italics] to find you, my true God, my sure sweetness. But where will the search lead me? Where am I to find you? If I find you beyond my memory, it means that I have no memory of you. How, then, am I to find you, if I have no memory of you?

This is the *other* El Camino Real, the real "Royal Road," toward which Saint Augustine directs his readers. But it is a road pointing ever inward and upward, away from the concrete conditions of the sensible world. It is a road laid for mystics and for saints, but not for human beings who must, of necessity, live in this sensate and wayward world. It seems to be safe to say that the current writers of memoirs are not really following The Royal Road provided with inner road signs by Saint Augustine. They are not looking *up* from inside the courtyard of a sacred palace of memory. Instead, they are contemplating their own navels, or else their spiritual bellies, in search of something as secular as it is sacred, as inside themselves as it is *outside*. They seem to be seeking the synthesis, the alternation suggested by the beggar at the Town and Country Mall.

It is Kathryn Harrison's *The Kiss* that is most often cited as the most daring, and perhaps the most inner-directed, of the new memoirs. This "confession," written in the form of a novella, dramatizes the sexual affair Ms. Harrison had with her father during her college years. The book was endorsed by Robert Coles for its emotional honesty, but some critics condemned the book for its portrait of the father, still a practicing minister, and for its potential impact on Ms. Harrison's two young children. I took a personal interest in this book when it appeared because I had worked with both Ms. Harrison and her husband Colin when they were students in the Writers' Workshop at the University of Iowa. As a matter of fact, the two of them met in my classes. They became a very loving couple, and they both seemed to have remarkable moral senses. Colin Harrison, as I recall, was still a practicing Quaker. He wrote, in some of his stories, about the retarded children with whom he once worked. I had many conversations with him about contemporary affairs. I recall that one day, when we were discussing the reelection of Ronald Reagan by a tremendous landslide (in 1984), Colin suddenly said, "I'm tired of feeling guilty!" It was only then that I recognized just how much of a moral burden had been placed on the remnant of the "liberal" element in American society. Reagan's reelection, by such a huge margin, has allowed them to disengage from other people's problems and to consider their own individual problems. Kathryn Harrison, on the other hand, wrote very quiet stories about family life in Los Angeles. I remember that, during a concert at the university auditorium, which I attended with my daughter, Colin and Kathryn passed down, from a great number of rows behind me, their own opera glasses for my daughter to use.

I receive, every Christmas, a card from them, always with a picture of their happy-seeming two children building snowmen.

I took my time in reading Kathryn's *The Kiss*.

Jill Ker Conway, in her recent consideration of the memoir form, *When Memory Speaks*, is ambivalent about the intentions behind Ms. Harrison's disclosures.

> Stories of incest victims usually receive favorable treatment because the child is presented as the innocent object of someone else's illicit desires. It is Harrison's acknowledgment of mutuality that has shocked her critics and has made *The Kiss* a riveting story, albeit one which leaves many issues of the author's identity and the familial relationships unresolved. The reader wonders whether she will ever be able to like other women, and thus like herself in later life, or whether she'll remain as exclusively focused on bonds with men as she was in her twenties.

It is of interest to note that in 1994, several years before publication of *The Kiss*, Ms. Harrison contributed an essay to a book called *A Tremor of Bliss: Contemporary Writers on the Saints*. Here again, Robert Coles was enthusiastic in his introduction. Once again, Ms. Harrison wrote about deeply personal matters. In her essay, "Catherine Means Pure," about Saint Catherine of Siena, Ms. Harrison confronts her own complex religious background—Jewish, Christian Scientist, Catholic—as well as the meaning of her own name. In this essay are some of the same themes that are given greater dramatization in *The Kiss*: a spiritually transcendent experience with a practitioner of Christian Science whose laying on of hands caused "the top of my skull . . . to be opened by a sudden, revelatory blow." And: "Mysteriously, unexpectedly, this stranger had ushered me into an experience of something I cannot help but call rapture. I felt myself separated from flesh, and from all earthly things. I felt myself no more

. . . .

corporeal than the tremble in the air over a fire. . . ." Finally, there are the comparisons between Ms. Harrison and Saint Catherine of Siena, who share the same name: "She wanted to do all her suffering on earth so that she would be spared purgatory. *This will make you pure*, I used to think when I made myself throw up." And again:

> No one believed more firmly in Catherine's debasement than did Catherine. Determined that she be the least among mortals, so also by the topsy-turvy logic of Christian salvation—she would be assured of being the greatest. In her vision of Christ, it is Catherine alone who stands beside Him as His bride. To earn that place was exhausting beyond mortal ability. Catherine would guide me to the salvation I sought. Inhumanly, she had triumphed over mortal limitations, over hunger, fatigue, and despair. She had seen demons and fought them off. And I would use her to fashion my solitary and simple faith. Sin. A term long ago borrowed from archery: to miss the mark.

Such spiritual longings are at the basis of Ms. Harrison's *The Kiss*. Simply put, like Saint Augustine, and like Saint Catherine, Ms. Harrison has gone deep into her memories of her own debasement in order to connect with what Augustine called the place "beyond memory" in order to reach a transcendent level. And Ms. Harrison does manage to reach this level, even in so secular and sociological a memoir as *The Kiss*. By exploring into such a deeply hidden part of her memory, she seems to have found something transcendent that she has brought into the outside world, in full view of her children. Once again, like the beggar at the exit of the Town and Country Mall, there is suggested the principle of *alternation*, of *integration* between the inner and the outer. Ms. Harrison's critics tend to ignore the mystical threads that parallel the sexual theme of the book. Besides the experience with the Christian Scientist, at the end of the book there is a dream about the writer's dead mother, who had caused her daughter so much pain:

> Yet she doesn't disappear, she is luminously real. With the split consciousness that sometimes characterizes a dream I remark to my sleeping self that perhaps my mother's spirit is really with me, that I can't have fabricated a presence so convincing simply by virtue of longing . . . We look into each other's eyes more deeply than we ever did in life, and for much longer. Our eyes don't move or blink, they are no more than a few inches apart. As we look, all that we have ever felt but have never said is manifest. Her youth and selfishness and misery, my youth and selfishness and misery. Our loneliness. The ways we betrayed each other. In this dream I feel that at last she knows me, and I her. I feel us stop hoping for a different daughter and a different mother.

Both women, here, seem to have located, in one integrated memory, the ultimate source of love.

How beautiful my mother and I are.

III

Jill Ker Conway, in her *When Memory Speaks*, attempts to offer insights into the entrenched cultural patterns that seem to be beneath the rise of the memoir form. She sees the sources of it in the rise of feminism over the past three decades and its formal patterns moving outside the self and into the public world. She reminds us:

> Whether we are aware of it or not, our culture gives us an inner script by which we live our lives. The main acts for the play come from the way our world understands human development; the scenes and the characters come from our families and socialization, which provide the pattern for investing others with emotional significance; and the dynamics of the script come from whatever our world defines as success or achievement.

Ms. Conway sees different patterns for men and women. "For men," she says, "the overarching pattern for life comes from adaptations of the story of the epic hero in classical antiquity." That is, the quester-hero must accomplish, through use of his own will, a feat of purposeful endurance or of victory over some adversary. Women, in contrast, have been traditionally assigned to writing narratives about their relation to God or to their households. "The secular forms of women's narratives emerge," according to Ms. Conway, "in the bourgeois preoccupation with romantic love, marriage, family and property." But over the past three decades, it seems there has been an erosion, or else a merging, of these two separate domains. Thus Kathryn Harrison can write an essay about Saint Catherine of Siena, and then follow this with a memoir about her own sexual adventures with her father, a quest-memoir about the road to parental love. But while Ms. Conway's paradigm may have once had authenticity in the world as it once *was*, an even more radical argument can be made for the kind of world, both inside and outside, that exists *now*. Perhaps it is only the beggar/philosopher who stands at the exit to the Town and Country Mall, who can open up insights into this new world for us. Or, perhaps, it is time for his black brother to instruct us in this mystery.

This past winter, a seventy-one-year-old homeless black man named Arthur Bell, was found nearly frozen on the streets of Brooklyn, New York. He kept maintaining, to a social worker named Maria Mackin, that he had once been a celebrated ballet dancer in New York and in Paris. The social worker, who was initially doubtful of his story, began checking the facts suggested to her. Bell's story was picked up by the Associated Press, reaching a much wider audience, and a black minister in Florida, who knew Bell's sister, contacted her and other members of the homeless man's family. *Jet* magazine later reported that Bell was later introduced to his brother, a successful businessman in suburban New Rochelle, and later to his five sisters in Florida. He had not seen them for forty years. Then the deeper story came out. Fifty-seven years before, the young Arthur Bell had fled his Florida home to follow his dream to become a ballet dancer. He had run away because his restrictive fundamentalist family in Tampa, Florida, made it difficult for him to achieve his secular dream. In 1950, Bell had premiered in "Illuminations" in the New York City Ballet. He danced, later, with the Ballet de la Tour Eiffel in Paris and achieved some fame. But, apparently, between the late 1950s and 1997, while the Civil Rights movement had brought prosperity to a great number of black people with comparable dreams, Bell's life became increasingly desperate. He had been homeless for several decades, sustained only by his memories of what he *had* been. His retreat into the *inside* of himself, where he kept his memories alive, resulted from the prolonged uncertainty of the *outside* world. But what he had preserved inside himself soon became, through the ministrations of the mass media, a portrait of the millions of other nameless and homeless men and women who also function as abstractions in the outside world.

Bell's true brother, the man at the exit to the Town and Country Mall, would know this instinctively. He knows that in the famous Silicon Valley, south on El Camino Real, among the rising number of technocrats and entrepreneurs, there is a similar sense of fragmentation. This new elite finds that it has more in common with its peers, worldwide, who use the same technocratic vocabulary, fly on the same airplanes, shop in the same airport malls, use the same hotels in New York, Chicago, Paris, Tokyo, Berlin, London, than they have in common with the people along the road to the north and south of them. A man wearing the usual business suit has his shoes shined by an Asian man in the lobby of an airport while he uses a cellular telephone to cement a business deal. He has no reason to even look at the Asian man shining his shoes until the job is done. The women in this elite are guarded from the haphazard intrusions of Eros by the growing number of company sexual-harassment codes. There is a growing tribe of affluent people, called "Eagles," who employ the new technology to enhance their mobility. Once connected to the workplace by the Internet, such people can make very comfortable homes for themselves away from the cities, in the small towns of Vermont, New Hampshire, Maine, or else in Iowa, Illinois, or even Kansas. They tend to live among, but *above*, the old-time residents of these small towns. The suburbs are now being abandoned for the exurbs, and the one-time locals feel displaced by their much better educated and much more affluent neighbors. There are the beginnings of tensions between the generations, as medical science allows older people to live longer, healthier lives, and collect more Social Security, at the expense of much younger people whose labor will pay for these benefits. Prosperity has been polarized, with great wealth concentrated in fewer and fewer hands. The institution of the nation-state is rapidly being replaced by global corporate ties under invisible managements. The middle class is frightened. The poor no longer exist as human beings. Europe is becoming one Federated Nation, while the demographics of the United States are changing relentlessly. Information is everywhere, but there is less and less of it with any substance. Private events that used to have tragic implications—the O. J. Simpson saga, the Atlanta Olympics bombing, the death of Princess Diana, the murder of Jon Benet Ramsey, the moral hollowness of Bill Clinton—are now treated as farce. Frank Sinatra is dead, and *Seinfeld* is going off the air. On a more personal level, a radically new type of human being is appearing—one who employs language only as a means to the negotiation of self-interested ends, with no regard for either truth or the consequences of his untruths because the language that is used is no longer grounded in a consistent sense of *self*. We say only what we *have* to say to get through each day.

Confronted on all sides by such radical trends, it is only predictable that the remnants of the individual self would need to take refuge within personal memories, within Saint Augstine's "belly of the soul." Arthur Bell, the Town and Country Mall man's brother, was himself a very wise man. He held fiercely onto the hidden high point of his life, even while he remained homeless in the world outside himself.

IV

At each stop along El Camino Real are narratives that have been stored in memory, narratives eager to be told, almost to any pedestrian. An Arab American who runs a flower shop has become an expert in observing the

. . . .

cynical, "romantic," manipulations employed by his customers. If you give him time, he will detail the many ploys they impose on the fragile red and pink blossoms he sells. If you give him even more time, he will draw his own experiences into the narrative ("My wife left me three times, and she came back three times. I took her back three times, but I put my property in my mother's name. My wife can't get shit! She's American and she's *crazy*. This is a garbage culture, man! A *garbage* culture!"). Such stories, living at almost each stop along The Royal Road, are being forged by newly arrived immigrants—Koreans, Ethiopians, Hindu, Caribs, Chinese, Spanish. At an automobile-repair shop, south on that road toward San Jose, a Chinese customer sits politely while complaining and complaining and complaining to a white male clerk about the shoddy repairs that have been made on his car. The reserved middle-aged clerk periodically breaks into the monologue with an offer to correct a specific mistake for free. The Chinese man ignores him. Intent on saving face, and knowing that the clerk has already conceded error, the Chinese man sits passively. He alternates, instead, between stoical silence and the refrain of complaints. North of them, at the checkout counter of a huge state-of-the-art copy center, an elderly black woman slowly inspects the pile of old black-and-white photographs that has just been copied. She holds her place at the usually efficient counter, against all the other customers behind her, to offer stories to the patient clerk about the children and the grandchildren in the pictures, as well as stories about their ancestors in the South. Further north of this place, at a bus stop, two people waiting for a bus give directions to a driver who is lost. One of the two is a black man, with the badge of city bus driver on his coat, who directs the lost driver through a complicated network of turns, so as to place the driver just at the door he is seeking. His fixation is on the "style" of the arrival. But the woman, a Chinese, points out a much more practical route to the destination. Two ethnic ethics are in competition, both for the benefit of the lost driver. Further south of them, inside another flower shop, a middle-aged white female, also a clerk, fantasizes about a lost love who has the same name as the man who is buying flowers. She swears that she once loved this black man, truly loved him, and will love him forever. She keeps vowing to seek out his relatives, and track him down one day, over in San Francisco. She keeps insisting that true love lasts forever.

What prevents such stories from having a wider audience? Why do they remain imprisoned in private memories?

This past winter, a Green Bay Packer star named Reggie White destroyed his career, and lost a job with CBS Sports, by making what was called a "racist speech" to the Wisconsin State Assembly in Madison. His condemnation of homosexuals was the least offensive part of the speech. Even more controversial was his assessment of the "talents" given by God to each race. Black people were gifted at worship and celebration, the ordained minister told the legislators. "If you go to a black church, you see people jumping up and down because they really get into it. White people are good at organizing," he said. "You guys do a good job of building businesses, and you know how to tap into money." "Hispanics," he went on, "are gifted in family structure, and you can see a Hispanic person, and they can put 20, 30 people in one house. Asians are gifted inventors and can turn a television into a watch. Indians are gifted in spirituality," he added. "When you put all of that together, guess what it makes? It forms a complete image of God."

While Mr. White will not be working for CBS Sports in the near future, his blunt remarks do raise a certain issue that touches the trend under consideration here. While the ideology of equality is a benevolent construct, and while considerations of "political correctness" may help alleviate certain ethnic/sexual tensions, it may be helpful to abandon both concepts and attempt to view human experience from what has been roundly condemned as a "racist" perspective. It may well be that the *ideology* of equality, with its rhetorical insistence on "sameness," tends to obscure some fundamental *differences*, the examination of which may provide a badly needed perspective on this present moment in the culture.

The one "sameness" that applies to each member of the human race is the fact of death, man's fate, as a given, as the fundamental end of life. Death is the great equalizer. But what is not equal is the range of responses to the ethical problem of *what should survive death*. This issue is ethical in the deepest possible sense because attempts at solving it are the basis of all great literature (from the *Upanishads* of the ancient Hindu to the *Epic of Gilgamesh* of the ancient Babylonians to the story of the Flood in the Book of Genesis), and of all great religions. Each historical society, if it is to achieve personality, and if it is to provide a philosophical or a religious orientation for its members, must wrestle with the fact of death, and with what should survive it, in order to project an ethical system, a *meaning*, that will survive death, whether in this world or in some other. Among the Hindu, for example, *being* is to survive by stripping all the mortal qualities from the self; the deathless is to be attained by removing that which lives.

The idea of reincarnation in other forms of life evolved out of this core belief. Among the Chinese, the family survives death, linking the ancestors in
the world of the spirit with its living members on the earth. The Japanese
have adapted this ethical system to their own needs, except that among
them the *ki*, the life force itself, is what survives death. The ancient Egyp-
tians invested the *ka*, the mystic double of a person, with the capacity to
survive among the spirits, while in this world the cult of the kingdom of
Egypt lived on. Among the ancient Greeks, the myth of the exemplary person survived death. This idea was adapted by the Romans, and centuries
later found an echo in Hegel's philosophy of history. Among the Muslims,
the inhabitants of the ancient Levantine world (from which Augustine of
Hippo emerged), the consensus of the Faithful survived, the unity of those
who have received the same spirit, in the Kingdom of Heaven. In sharp
contrast to all these ethical systems, Western peoples view the personal
will, the "inner script" described by Ms. Jill Ker Conway, as the agent of
survival. From this point of view, a person's will becomes the causative
agent of one's spiritual fate. This is an ethic based on actions in this world,
the creation of cognitive institutions—businesses, churches, family lines,
fortunes, foundations—that will impose one's will on the future.

These may be some of the archetypal ethical patterns beneath Mr. Reggie White's cloudy stereotypes. It is apparent to me that these diverse ethical systems are now coming into proximity, if not into conflict, along El
Camino Real. This recent shrinkage of the world into a single Royal Road
is one of the sources, I believe, of the fear leading to the massive retreat
from the public square and into the gated community of the self. There is
a growing fear of the unknown along that Great Road. It needs to be em-
phasized that El Camino Real, following the changing demographic patterns of the nation, has become a veritable supermarket of free-floating
ethical systems, some of them degraded now beyond easy recognition.
People have retreated deep into themselves, trying desperately to connect
with the fading, familiar forms of "home." This in itself is a noteworthy
expression of *one* side of the principle of alternation, but the completion
of the principle, the return to the *outside* of the self, is not an easy thing to
do, especially without the recognition that the habits of mind beneath all
such efforts are *different*. They are invisible. But still they exist, as do the
stories that can be filtered through them. They can only be drawn into
greater focus through personal encounters that take place outside the
gated community of the self.

But this is the great risk that many of us are unwilling to chance now, in those dangerous places outside of ourselves, along The Royal Road.

Several days ago the new Hindu government of India began testing nuclear weapons. I had been reading the works of Mahatma Gandhi for several months before the first explosions, and after the second testing I began reading him much more carefully. The appropriation of Western physics by India seemed to make meaningless much of what the Mahatma taught the world about India. "Strength lies in the absence of fear, not in the quality of flesh and muscle we have on our bodies. . . . The Gujarati equvalent for civilization means 'good conduct.' India has nothing to learn from anybody else . . . .To arm India on a large scale is to Europeanize it. Then her condition will be just as pitiable as that of Europe. This means, in short, that India must accept European civilization. . . ."

These quotations are from Gandhi's first book, *Hind Swaraj*, published in 1908. In this book he outlined a tactic that, he predicted, would drive out the English and their civilization and liberate modern India. Things seem now to not have worked out as Gandhi has planned. Still, the vitality of his core conviction, Swaraj (self-rule), drawn by him from the Hindu *Upanishades* of 1000 B.C. and *The Bhagaved Gita*, had the power to influence the many millions of occupied India and activists like Martin Luther King. The concept, which preceded by 1,000 years the meditation on freedom by Plato and Aristotle, offered a solution to the division between the outside and the inside that has since been wrestled with by Plato, Plotinus, Saint Augustine, and even John Locke. It suggested, almost 3,000 years ago, the same principle of alternation conveyed by the beggar/philosopher stationed by the exit at the Town and Country Mall: "Let the words of my mouth and the meditation of my heart be acceptable in thy sight," as the Christians would say.

Gandhi explained his interpretation of Swaraj in a dual sense, one physical and one spiritual, working together to achieve the same end. To rule over territory or even to rule over people, one must first rule over one's self, over one's own soul. One must, first, free oneself psychologically of all illusions and fears. The highest level of consciousness comes when our individual being is *one* with all being. The freest person, then, is the one who sees all being in himself and himself in all being. The engagement with this Royal Road, which leads to self-knowledge and to unity-in-diversity, Gandhi argued in his *Hind Swaraj*, was the only practical road to Indian independence. He repeated this lesson all his life. In speak-

. . . .

ing against the practice of untouchability he said, once again reemphasizing Swaraj:

> Hinduism has sinned in giving sanction to untouchability. It has degraded us, made us the pariahs of the (British) Empire. . . .What crimes for which we condemn the (British) Government as satanic, have not we been guilty of toward our untouchable brethern? . . . It is ideal to talk of Swaraj so long as we do not protect the weak and the helpless or so long as it is possible for a simple Swarajist to injure the feelings of any individual. Swaraj means not a single Hindu or Muslim shall for a moment arrogantly think that he can crush with impunity meek Hindus or Muslims. Unless this condition is fulfilled we will gain Swaraj only to lose it the next moment. We are not better than the brute until we have purged ourselves of the sins we have committed against our weaker brothers. . . . I do not want to attain Moksha [Salvation, merger with God] I do not want to be re-born. But if I have to be re-born, I should be born as an untouchable so that I may share their sorrows, suffering and the affronts leveled at them in order that I may endeavor to free myself and them from that miserable condition.

Since the practice of Swaraj is an individual discipline, Gandhi resolved the *inward* problem for himself by creating a new word, Harijans ("Children of God"), that would remove the stigma of untouchability. And then, as an *outward* expression of the freedom that resulted, he adopted an untouchable girl, Lakshmi, into his own family at the Satyagraha Ashram.

It remains to be seen just how much of this ancient and muscular ethic remains after the explosion of nuclear bombs derived from Western physics. But it seems to me that if India has turned to nuclear force in order to calm its fears of its neighbors, some other people will need to return to Gandhi's advocation of the uses of soul force. As he demonstrated, this is the work of solitary individuals. And since writers are the most solitary and self-aware of people, it seems to be our responsibility to use this period of inward-turning, of re-identification with our own ethical systems, the grain in our own wood, as a preparation for moving *out* of ourselves, having conquered our own fears of the rope that resembles a snake, or the beggar who threatens, to see what else in the outside world can be reclaimed. This is only a return to the principle of alternation suggested by Gandhi and by Martin Luther King, as well as by the beggar/philosopher who stands at the exit to the Town and Country Mall. Gloria Steinem, an early leader of the feminist movement, called it "a revolution from within." The prenuclear Hindi called it simply Swaraj.

There is, finally, one very important aesthetic consideration that should not be overlooked. It may well be that the conventional literary forms—the short story, the novel, and even the memoir—are unsuited to deal adequately with the new realities (global, demographic, economic, interpersonal) evolving just outside our gated communities. It should be recalled that these old forms grew out of specific cultural changes, primarily in Europe—the rise of a middle class, the consolidation of the nation-state, the invention of the printing press, the focus on the individual as worthy of emotional exploration, the exploration by Europeans of other parts of the world; but most important of all, *settled habits of mind which formed a psychological consensus in favor of specific forms*. Now, the concrete conditions of the outside world are changing at an increasingly accelerated rate of speed. Perhaps the old forms will not suffice to capture the new habits of mind, the new fears, we are obliged to confront every day. If this is truly the case, for my own part I still draw inspiration from a speech made by Ralph Ellison when he was awarded, in 1953, the National Book Award for his novel *Invisible Man*. Ellison said:

> We who struggle with form and with America should remember Eidothea's advice to Menelaus when in the *Odyssey* he and his friends are seeking their way home. She tells him to seize her father, Proteus, and to hold him fast, 'however he may struggle and fight. He will turn into all sorts of shapes to try you,' she says, 'into all the creatures that live and move upon the earth, into water, into blazing fire; but you must hold him fast and press him all the harder. When he is himself, and questions you in the same shape that he was when you saw him in his bed, let the old man go; and then, sir, ask which god it is who is angry, and how you shall make your way homewards over the fish-giving sea?'

I think it is time for me to go outside and look for another story, a new one, along The Royal Road.

The Dog of Memory

. . . .

by

ALVIN GREENBERG

Why a man in his midsixties, happily ensconced in the great love of his later life, should be concerned with remembering his first kiss, I can't imagine, except that he's read several times lately in various versions of the popular press that one never forgets one's first kiss, and he's certain that the conventional wisdom, as always, must be on to something. He— well, OK, I—can't recall exactly where I read (or was it heard?) about the unforgettableness of the first kiss, but that's the least of my concerns. The fact is, I *have* forgotten it. The fact also is that given my present life, I shouldn't even *care* that I've forgotten it. Was it such a big deal, that first unremembered kiss, so important that I should be letting the conventional wisdom get its cliché-stained hands around my wrinkly throat? Well, yes, you bet: that kiss was a long time coming—I wasn't exactly a kissable kid—and by no means an immediate prelude to subsequent smooching. It was a lonely lighthouse, that first kiss, on the romantically barren beach of my youth, a larger-than-life statue, like Rodin's (well, no, surely not at all like Rodin's): *The Kiss*. And although it has not been a big deal for a very long time now—the big deal at this age being instead the state of memory itself—it is still with some dismay that I confess to not remembering it. No wonder I started out here trying to avoid looking foolish and ignorant by giving the problem to some anonymous third-person character.

Blame it on the creeping forgetfulness of age, time's relentless deterioration of mind and body, except that again the conventional wisdom—this time with a fair amount of support from scientific research—tells us that's not the way it works. It's recent, short-term memory that's the first to go, rather than those fragments of the more distant past that have long since

79

taken up permanent residence in the tenements of the brain, decrepit squatters upon whom ownership eventually descends. I still remember the first telephone number we had when I was a child (MElrose 5 1 1 3), as well as a headlong dive off a park swing when I was two or three, with my step-mother and grandmother both looking on (or, more likely, not looking), as well as . . . well, you get the point. The beaches of my mind—not unlike your own, I'm sure—are littered with the detritus the tides of the past have swept up. And however much you or I value those glittering bits of sea glass, no beachcomber who ever passes that way is likely to find it inter-esting enough to bother to stop for a second look.

And somewhere back there, half or wholly buried in those sands of time no doubt, washed over decade after decade by the tides of forgetful-ness, lies my first kiss. Well, no, not my first kiss, of course, but the mem-ory of my first kiss. Or rather, *a* memory of my first kiss, which may or may not have much to do with that first kiss itself or with the memory of it as it resides in the mind of my cokisser, assuming that she (whoever she is) is still alive (as indeed both I and the statistics on male/female longevity would like to think she is). But where is it? Since being informed that one never forgets one's first kiss—no more than one forgets one's first-grade teacher (and I remember Mrs. Norcross as clearly as I recall the burnt English muffin I just had for breakfast)—I have gone over the territory with the industriousness of one of those old men one sees sweeping the beach with metal detectors in search of other sorts of treasures and gener-ally, I presume, with no more luck than I've had. And though I've turned up quite a lot of old stuff, some of it fairly interesting (never mind now) and much of it no more identifiable than a rusted nail that yields no indi-cation of what it was ever pounded into, that first kiss has yet to start my past detector clicking.

So what? you say. What difference does it make? Believe me, I'd be the first to join you in that shrug of indifference. What difference *could* it pos-sibly make at this late date whether it was Gladys in the seventh grade or Diane in the eighth? But the fact is—blame it on the pressure of the con-ventional wisdom, blame it on age's desire to recapture youth, blame it on the current fad for nostalgia, blame it, if you want, on the weather, since it's in the peculiar climatic conditions of the past that, like Gulf storms swirling up the Mississippi Valley to drench the great North where I now live, today's storms are often born—*I* care.

Not because of the kiss itself, which, given a bumbling adolescence that I generally do my best not to remember, I can't imagine having been espe-

· · · · · · · · · ·

cially romantic or even successful. (Did I hit her lips on target? bump noses? lock braces? for that matter, was I the kisser or the kissee?) No, surely not because of the kiss, which clearly didn't make much impact on my life (or I'd remember it as well as I remember the emergency appendectomy whose subsequent complications set me aside from most of my ten-year-old buddies for the better part of a year). Most definitely not because of the kiss, which in the history of kisses since was at best a first small drop of rain preceding the downpour—well, OK, the afternoon shower—to come, a damp peck on the cheek that serves at best to make one look up at the swollen skies. Who, indeed, could care about such a kiss?

Memory, however, is another matter, especially when the world is boxing your ears with its insistence.

Speak, Memory, orders the title of Nabokov's memoir, as if it were a dog that'd sit up and recite the past for a Milk-Bone or an ear scratch. But memory's a slyer mutt than that, not beyond perking up its ears, wagging its tail, and then nipping your fingers. And for a word of praise from its master it would just as soon dig up an imagined tale if it can't recall exactly where it buried that bone it thinks you're looking for.

■ ■ ■

When I was a college sophomore, someone—no, of course I don't remember who—taught me a trick for remembering an almost limitless number of words, an old mnemonic device that (as best I can recall) worked something like this. For each number from one to ten (or was it zero to nine?) you memorized a specific image: one was maybe oil, two was a table, three was a thimble, four a fountain, five a fish, six a sandwich, and so on. You get the alliterative point. And that's about all there was to it. You had your private basket of little hooks to carry with you wherever you went, just in case you were asked to hang a list of words up in the closet of your mind. Then, when someone gave you a word, you simply hooked it onto the pre-existing image or images to make a memorable picture. Instead of remembering *skunk* when you were given the first word in some interminable and insipid list, you visualized a skunk opening a can of 10w30. The weirder your mental image the better, the easier the recall. Needless to say, you didn't reveal that that was what you were doing; you just gave off a look of intense concentration, as if this were the intellectual equivalent of cleaning the Augean stables. By the time you got up to, say, number thirty-five on the list, and the word was, say, *brother*, you were picturing your brother with a thimble (for three, remember?) on his finger trying to pick up a dead fish. Who could forget that? You could easily do a hundred or more words if your audience had a vocabulary that was up to it. (Abstract words were a little trickier, but given the nature of my audiences that was rarely a problem.) You could recite the list as easily backward as forward, give out the words for numbers called at random or the number for a word selected at random. Women swooned. Men backed off in terror. It was a cheap parlor trick, but for a brief period in my life I loved it and would have gotten someone to shill for me at parties—"Hey, Al, show Sharon here that memory thing you do"—except that it was never necessary.

Funny, I haven't thought about that in twenty or thirty years. I'm surprised I still remember how it works—if, in fact, that *is* how it works.

There was a point to this, though.

Something about memory as a trained dog.

For entertainment purposes only.

■ ■ ■

The researchers of memory, those scientists who tweak the poor befuddled brain to see how and where it stores its stuff and by what sly devices and with what dubious accuracy it struggles to retrieve what it can—what should we call them? memorists? memorialists?—have long confirmed the conventional wisdom. No, not about the first kiss, although that's something that in my humble opinion they might profitably do some interesting research on, but about the more general notion that certain significant moments—e.g., one's first kiss—are embedded in one's memory forever, like fossils in limestone (or race forever around the maze of the brain's electric circuitry like a subway train with no conductor aboard and no scheduled stops). Where were you when FDR announced the attack on Pearl Harbor? ("A day that will live in infamy," I heard from the backseat of the family Chevy on the way home from a Sunday visit to my grandparents.) When JFK was assassinated? (In the midst of conducting a student conference in the mildewy stench, which I can still smell, of my basement office at the University of Kentucky.) King? Lennon? When Challenger exploded or Pan Am 103 went down over Lockerbie? When the secret of your birth was first revealed? When your spouse first confessed . . . ?

Well, some episodes are more personal than others, more traumatic, more, I'm sorry to say, memorable. And according to the professionals and the amateurs alike, a first kiss is supposed to be one of those.

Is there a difference, I wonder, between *memorable* and *unforgettable*? Is a memorable occasion the equivalent of an unforgettable face? (Remember that regular *Reader's Digest* article, "The Most Unforgettable Person I Ever Met"?) Or is there something subtly but significantly different here? Does the clear, direct, and audible—you can practically hum it—association of *memorable* with *memory* and *memorial* suggest itself as something so important that we would, if only we could, always choose to remember it, whereas the negative prefix of *unforgettable*, along with its antonymic root, implies that it's something that, were it possible, we'd be happier to forget? Do two negatives connote a dubious positive?

If my first kiss wasn't memorable, was it then forgettable? So utterly forgettable, so antonymically unrememberable, that I don't get to have access to a simple, inconsequential little thing like this that's apparently available to everyone else?

I whistle up the good dog memory.

"Fetch," I say.

She just sits and stares at me with those big, brown, Labrador eyes.

Eventually she tires of this. She did want to earn her biscuit, though. So she goes off and roots around out of my sight for a bit, then comes back with . . . ah, no. Please, not that one. I thought we'd buried that one deeper than any dog could dig. But she lays it at my feet anyway, all crusted with dirt and soggy where she's had her mouth around it.

This is not entertaining.

"OK," I say, "you still get your biscuit."

I'm a sucker for retrievers.

■ ■ ■

My high-school yearbook was called *The Remembrancer*, a name we took for granted at the time since that's what it had always been called, but that strikes me now as a little silly, phony, artificial, an almost embarrassing, high-schoolish (of course), made-up word that, nonetheless, makes its point, even grammatically. Obviously it speaks in its semantic root to memory, to remembering, that's what yearbooks are all about, but that clumsy suffix, that stuttering *-er* at the end, gives it an unexpectedly active role. It's not supposed to be a passive thing, this oversized volume with the heavily textured blue cover with its deeply incised gold title, its midcentury year, and its classical seal (*Sursum ad Summum*, it advised us: rise to the Highest). It wasn't meant to just lie there any more than we were, closed and unconsulted, gathering dust in the back of the closet or some far corner of the attic, boxed up and ignored. It's (as it expects us to be) a doer . . . er . . . er . . . er.

Grrr.

It nips at your ankles with all the usual things, of course: individual photos of the faculty and senior class and class officers; group photos against an identical background, on the steps to a side entrance, of all the homerooms from grade seven to grade eleven; carefully posed "action" photos of sports teams and thespians and newspaper editors; cutesy photos of the Best Dancers dancing, the Best Dressers all dressed up, the Most Popular and Mostly Likely to Succeed being popular and successful. It wants to play, and the name of its game is: when this you see, remember me. It's got its teeth into the toe end of an old sock and wants you to tug at the ankle end. And I'd love to, because somewhere in there—the Chess Club (not likely; almost all male), Eastern Star (hardly; no Jews), the Modern Dance Society (not impossible), the Latin Club (hmmm)—is the object, the subject, the coparticipant, the forgotten her of my first kiss. But as soon as I pull back, it lets go, and I'm left holding the limp elastic of an empty sock with a hole in its heel, a book of glossy pages full of faces and names in which I can't find *the* face, *the* name.

The autographs and scrawled greetings, the senior year farewells— "Lots O Luck," "Good knowing you," "Your friend," or the obsequious "To a great guy!"—don't provide a clue. Even if she'd signed in—and who knows, maybe she did—what was she going to say, after all, knowing that others would be opening those pages to inscribe their names as well: "To a swell kisser"? Not likely. Not even if it were true.

It's beginning to seem that *in* the past there are no clues *to* the past, that it's only in the present, if anywhere, in some still active corner of today's brain or upon a chance tomorrow meeting with herself, at which she recalls, at first sight of me (but what are the odds that she'd even remember me, aged and changed, bearded and balding?), that it was her first kiss too (but was it?), that we can find what we need of the past.

■ ■ ■

"The past," as H. E. Bates has said so poignantly in *The Go-Between*, "is another country." But they don't, as his story goes on to assert, "do things differently there." They don't *do* anything there. Whatever they did there, whatever we did there, is done. Finished, kaput, over with. A buried bone. I can't go back and join the Art League, try out for the football team, or raise my GPA. I can't, I am happy to say (and I hear this from others with some frequency as well, especially when it comes to those junior high and high school years), go back there at all. It is the Oakland of our lives: There is, as Gertrude Stein might have said, no longer any there there.

And yet, of course, although we can no longer take up residence there, the past inhabits us. It fills us, sometimes, like a populous city, its crowded street scenes and intimate interiors playing themselves passionately out on the strange inner screens of our minds, sometimes over and over again, and often whether we desire to sit through another showing or not. Disney never had such a captive audience, not even for the R-rated stuff. If we make our visits to that distant country it's only, as Blake would have it, as mental travelers. There's no need for passport and visa, for airline and hotel reservations, or visits to the currency exchange; we travel there on our own schedule or we're suddenly, unexpectedly transported there by some out-of-control inner travel agent. But in the land of the past we find we're spectators only, not participants. We're fluent in the language, but no one talks to us. They seem too preoccupied even to notice our presence, and they're not the least bit willing to take us on guided tours of the great monuments. I want to ask directions—"Can you tell me, please, how to get to The First Kiss?"—but my every effort is ignored as they go about doing exactly what they were doing on my last visit, what they've always done and always will be doing, acting—but it's no act—as if they don't understand a word of my strange language, although it has the same syntax, the same vocabulary, as theirs, rendering me—and in my very own past!—quite invisible.

It all feels like the snipe hunts of my childhood summer evenings, when we conned some younger kid into getting a bag and waiting quietly in the depths of the forest—a rather scraggly little woods, actually, although of course we needed to hype the danger level to make it into a test of bravery and endurance—while we drove the putative prey, the infamous snipe, in his or her direction for capture. So here I wait, the empty sack of my mind wide open and hungry for its catch, assuming that the good dog of memory is beating the bushes on my behalf to flush the quick rabbit of that first kiss out of hiding and send it hopping into my clutches. But all the while, just as the rest of us used to return to a game of kick-the-can in someone's backyard while our poor victim hunkered down in the growing dark, afraid to stay and embarrassed to return, the old dog is snoozing on the living-room carpet, a piece of polished shin bone lying beside her whitening muzzle and only the occasional twitching of her legs betraying any dream of the hunt. And I am still sitting in the dark, remembering nothing. Shamefaced, I have no choice but to leave that darkening forest, where vision grows more and more dim, and return to the lighted present.

■ ■ ■

So is there any sense asking *Where was I?* when it seems that the only valid question is *Where am I?* As Archimedes longed for the fulcrum that would enable him to weigh the world, the present is perhaps the only point of balance from which we can prise up the past and understand just how it weighs upon us. Or should we say, how it lifts us up (*Sursum ad Summum!*) on the other end of the seesaw of our lives? We are dogged throughout our lives by memories—the good, the bad, and the indifferent—but they're not our past, those memories, they're with us in the here-and-now; memories, unlike the remembered events, are not what we were but part of all we currently are. That first kiss: *c'est moi*—or so the memory of it would be if only I could find it.

But, of course, as every aging body can tell you (proving yet another piece of conventional wisdom: that time will tell), I am not what I was. And maybe that's what's so important for us about memory: what time deconstructs, memory attempts to reassemble. It's no parlor game after all; it's our very lives. Willed forgetfulness, the deliberate disremembering of pain or trauma, is surely understandable—who wants to suffer that again, even in thought?—but at the same time it's a hacking off of a significant chunk of who we are, a severing of flesh and bone, and generally no matter how hard we try, that phantom limb of the past still aches from time to time. It reasserts itself in the where-we-are, and not always with discomfort, either. Just as often, I'd say—more often, I'd hope—it throbs with the joy of old loves no longer physically at our side; with the elegant ease of events long past being folded into the fabric of our lives, like the long fly ball of my youth arcing down into deep left field out of the glare of the lights to settle comfortingly into my outstretched glove; with the solace of an old dog laying her heavy head in our lap, reminding us that she's always there whenever we want to play fetch, although there may be times when weariness or preoccupation or just plain forgetfulness prevents her from bringing back the exact bone we sent her off for.

"Remember the Van Wagenens"

. . . .

by
LYDIA DAVIS

The age of fifty, whether it is or not, looks very much like a halfway point. So this may be why—imagining rightly or wrongly that we are nel mezzo del camin di nostra vita—we find ourselves reconsidering our life (looking forward) and considering our life (looking back).

I quote this Italian not to show off my foreign-language ability, but because these are some of the few "memorized" words that tend to float into the forefront of my mind quite regularly, if not necessarily accurately. These particular words are sometimes followed by others no doubt even less accurate: *mi ritrovai in un' selva oscura.*

Dream about Mademoiselle Roser: She was in a small-town library, probably this one here in my town, but not resembling it. She had short straight white hair (she did not in actual life), she was very kempt and fashionable, rather small (she was large in actual life). I was very happy to see her there. At last I could tell her that I had grown up to be a translator, and was now in fact translating Proust, which would have to appear to her as a sort of pinnacle of a translator's career, whether it really is or not (the real pinnacle being, perhaps, the less popular Leiris, who may be, in fact, stylistically more accomplished than Proust, and doesn't a translator test her mettle on style rather than the whole conception or form of a work?). I realized that she might not remember me, but she would still be pleased that a pupil of hers was now translating French. She was an emphatic, exuberant, and generous person, with severe, high standards. I was very happy. Then I remembered that she had died.

87

I tell my mother I think Mlle Roser, though dead, can still see me and understand. She is shocked. "You don't really believe that!" But I do. I did not use to believe the dead lived on, but I have changed my thinking about that.

There was a hunt, last month, at the old school, for evidence of Mlle Roser. We went down into the basement, even into certain locked inner rooms behind the utility or shop rooms. There were no old boxes of that particular textbook. But back upstairs there were some letters and a few photographs. She was an impressive-looking woman. The photographs seemed to confirm my memory of her, but once I had seen them, I had to work hard to remember what it was I actually did remember, without the influence of the photographs.

When you think you will not remember something, you write it down, either in a notebook or on a handy piece of paper. You have many pieces of paper all over the house and in all sorts of pockets and bags with things written on them that you either don't remember or also remember—either do not have in your mind also or do have in your mind also. So the pieces of paper with writing on them supplement the living tissue of your memory, as though your usable, active memory goes beyond the bounds of your head out onto these pieces of paper.

Could one say that, in outward-moving circles (or planes—rectangles or squares), not only does the notebook supplement and represent the mind, but the desk also, then the study, the house, and the grounds of the house? (Stopping at the fence: beyond it, the street, the neighborhood and the town are no longer private spaces.)

Gaston Bachelard's *The Poetics of Space* is of course very important (though the translation is in spots unnecessarily abstract and obtuse). The verticality of the house; the rationality, the intellectuality of the attic; the darkness, the subterranean, the unconscious of the cellar.

Where would your oldest, your childhood friend be, after forty years of disappearance? When you locate her again, where is she? To your surprise, in Africa. But then you see the naturalness of it: where else would the material of the most essential old memories retreat, but to the continent that has always been so mysterious to you?

. . . .

Her name, too, is White, so now there is a light in the unconscious.

Her two younger sisters, being less essential, have retreated only as far as Massachusetts and Philadelphia.

The difference between the thing remembered (the landscape of memory) and the present-day reality (both of them existing). The difference between the street of the childhood memory—and the street now. The house then—and the house now. White and her sisters then, on Crescent Street—and now: in Massachusetts, Philadelphia, and . . . Nigeria. Their grandmother's Whately house then—in the midst of vast fields—and now: crowded by other houses. My other friend August next door then—eating a lamb chop at her kitchen table (clear as day in my mind)—and now, in Paris (less clear). But both the thing remembered and what there is now exist. Only, one exists only in my brain and the other out there for other people to see, too.

The memories exist physically in the brain cells. A smell opens a pathway to the memory of a canvas bookbag that I haven't remembered for years. At least I don't remember that I have remembered it, and yet the cells containing it have sat there in my brain for years.

Why is there any need to find them again (childhood friend and grammar book)? To tie together that past and this present, but also that self that I was then with this self now? Is it once again a question of saying, Yes, I do exist, and Yes, I did exist all along?

Trying out the idea that this particular past does not matter anyway. Another person has another past, that matters to her. But that doesn't matter in any absolute way, any more than mine absolutely matters. She also wants to find her childhood friends. But I could exchange mine for hers; mine have no more weight than hers. It is all circumstantial and accidental. Which is why other people's "earliest" memories are so often banal: they have no objective interest, and yet their authors are bent on "truthfully" reporting them.

William Bronk writing it over and over again: that we are each only temporary manifestations of Life. Or at least, this is what I want to think he is writing, and so this is how I remember it.

.   .   .   .

That the dead are still "with us": it started, anyway, with Mlle Roser. I say to my mother, quite sincerely (I am trying again to remember it correctly), that I believe Mlle Roser, whom my mother remembers joining more than once for dinner and for some sort of theatrical performance in Paris, and who died some years ago, is still alive in some form and taking an interest in what I may write about her and in what I may "do" with my French. I say to my mother that I believe Mlle Roser is still aware of some things, and she says in a shocked tone, "Are you serious?" In her tone is not mere interest or curiosity, as I would prefer, but incredulity and a hint of scorn— this notion of mine, if sincere, is ridiculous, even hysterical (or am I mis- reading her tone: is this really the urgency of an old woman who can't afford to waste precious minutes of her remaining life reacting to insincere statements?).

It is sure that the dead, in any case, live in memory, in the recesses of the mind. But seem to be outside the mind. Just as a childhood landscape re- membered seems to be outside, as it was really outside at the time. That landscape was outside me at the time, but is inside me now. No one sees it but I. Others see what is there now instead of that landscape (what is there being usually a more crowded landscape).

The dead living on, "really": in the case of Mlle Roser, is this impression stronger because she was a teacher, and a teacher of young children, there- fore someone overseeing, someone taking command and assuming re- sponsibility for the many young lives who passed through her hands? So that even "up there" she would still feel somehow responsible?

Or is this impression produced by the force of my desire, now that it is too late, to tell her what those early days of her teaching now mean to me? Including the textbook, which I can't find anywhere?

Or is it that when one reaches a certain age of being older than so many people, instead of being younger than so many (having so many elders), one wishes to bring back a figure who was not only much older but also a teacher, therefore an appointed guide and guardian, in at least one area (the French language)? Is it because the guides and teachers, the guard- ians, appointed and unappointed, are dropping away, every day?

The French grammar is called *Le Français par la Méthode Directe* by Robin and Bergeaud. It is a slim book with a red cover, published over fifty years ago by Librairie Hachette, and I am looking everywhere for a copy, even in poor condition.

We focus always, and over and over each day, on the details of our par-
ticularity (I love his particular handwriting whenever I see it) when we
(and it all) are really just happenstantial (we love what we come to love,
but we might easily never have come to it: I would love his Bronx accent,
but he doesn't have one). Am I more lovable, objectively, than that young
Hasidic woman standing in the subway? If I were objectively more lovable, then that young Hasidic man would love me instead.

My impression is that almost any one poem of William Bronk's that I
could find would say what I am thinking so many of his poems say—what
I prefer to remember and think they say—but that is not quite true.

Living Instead

> Nothing much we can do about it so we live
> the way old bones and fossils lived, the way
> long-buried cities lived: we live instead
> —just as if and even believing that here
> and finally now, ours could be the real world.

This is not quite the thought I was after: I quote it "instead."

There are certain things I think I "ought to" remember, if I am to be a responsible representative of my time and generation, but where there
should be a memory there is often a blank. Commonest example I give myself: the Bay of Pigs. I never wanted to remember anything about it. The
Cuban Missile Crisis. I erased understanding of these "current" events
even as I learned about them. I wanted to wipe the slate clean. To have a
"clear mind"? How to have a clean slate and still have a reliable memory
bank for reference, and be responsible to succeeding generations?

Hypogeum: the subterranean part of an ancient building. The doubled re-
moval in that idea.

One who shares a past with you loses his memory: what happens to you?
That past is suddenly wiped out, or in danger of being wiped out, or ren-
dered meaningless, or less meaningful, or even more accidental (unnecessary) than it was. If suddenly only you remember it, because Father does
not (Father sitting there in his plastic chair with his mouth open). As
though it were a geometrical figure that has lost its depth, its third dimension, the legs it stood on.

. . . .

This memory of mine could be exchanged for any other memory of mine. Any other person's memory, even. Let me tell you something I remember from my childhood: and this is not true, it is someone else's memory, or a story I read that someone else made up. It is fiction. You hear it as my memory. That does not matter; you take it as my memory. Even I may not know it is not mine.

Past gone, like a building gone, or a tree.

A building is gone leaving no trace on the ground, especially no trace in the air—of course—and yet up there, in the air, many lives unfolded.

And then with a certain belief in magic, we think lives that unfolded within walls have left physical traces on those stones, and is that why we pick up a shard of stone from a ruin, or a handful of soil from Greece, and take it away in our pocket? Is it just a belief in magic, or a superstition? Is it laughable?

What about the man who has a fireplace he has built himself incorporating a stone from every state in the continental U.S.? It is in some sense magical for him, full of potency—those stones are more than ordinary stones in a "fieldstone" fireplace. But they have no intrinsic value, and to someone who doesn't know, they have no value: here comes the wrecker and scatters and shatters the stones, the one from Arizona over there and the one from South Dakota here, gone. They have value only for the builder, who knows them, who has invested them with value. The way we invest our pets with personality, character, with a larger personality and character than a stranger can see, upon first meeting our pet.

A tree is taken down. It leaves no trace in the air, though it was up there in that air for so many years, often a hundred or more.

The vegetable garden that was planted in the same place by this roadside every year is not planted anymore because the gardener grew too old and too feeble. So there is just another twelve-foot square of lawn now, along with the rest of the lawn. The third dimension—the growth several feet up into the air—and the complexity, the tangle and chaos, is gone now.

On the top floor, this time, a floor with lower ceilings, the servants' floor, of a house on Gardner Street in Providence: open the doors of a cabinet, pull out a drawer, lift a cover from a box, and there you see stones labeled as coming from places in Egypt, in Greece, other countries (Persia?) collected many decades ago, even a century ago, by this family with money traveling abroad.

. . . .

But having said this, I am not sure the house was on Gardner Street after all, or even if there is such a street.

Was that top floor the part of the house equivalent to rationality, or to memory?

If you don't know this house here is Mozart's birthplace, you are not interested, even though you walk right past it, a great lover of Mozart.

If you do know, you stand before it filled with a number of emotions and thoughts, including awe.

On the other hand, if you have made a mistake, and are standing in front of the wrong house thinking it is Mozart's house, your thoughts and emotions are exactly the same as if you stood in front of the correct house. Are they just as valuable? You will come back from your trip abroad and tell someone about the experience—your thoughts and emotions included—and that experience will make a difference to you as your life goes on, and will perhaps make a difference to the person or the many people you tell about your experience in front of Mozart's house, and it won't matter that it was the wrong house. It won't matter unless you find out it was the wrong house. Then in your own eyes you will feel you did not really have the experience you thought you had. Your experience was false, and had no value.

The example of Mozart's house is a bad example, because it must have a plaque on it, and even perhaps colorful banners, and crowds going in and out. But there are other houses that are unmarked, the former habitations of other much-loved people. And there are other places in front of which we have stood feeling awe that will never be given plaques, such as the stationery shop in Paris where Samuel Beckett bought his note cards. "That man put his foot on this very threshold once."

Not only that the dead are still alive, but also, sometimes, the conviction that the past still exists. But I can't tell if this is because I am so fully imagining it (and have returned so often in my imagination to the same place and time) or because it "really" still exists—not in "our" space and time but in some other dimension.

It has been quite a few years that I have been looking, sporadically, for my early friend White and for that grammar book with the red cover. Now I have found out where both of them are, though I haven't yet contacted my friend and do not yet have the grammar book in my possession. I have the address of one, and, of the other, the many pages constituting a photo-copy. Paper, again, is replacing or standing in for the real thing, or signal-ing the real thing, or providing me with a handy reminder of the real thing. Though of course one of the real things, in this case, is itself largely paper.

Why do I want the past (the material contained in my memory) to live on in the present? Why do I want evidence of it now? And why do I want someone else to know, too? Why am I not content to leave it where it is and remember it in solitude? Revisit it from time to time (this time it is a dining room with massive dark furniture in Vienna, and there is a block puzzle on the dining-room table)? (It could be the ripe cherries from the cherry trees in the enclosed back garden of a house in Graz, and the gar-den itself.) (Are the memories of "foreign" experiences more concentrated and more potent for me because these experiences were so unlike what I grew up with before and after, or because they were so much richer sensu-ally?) And if you give a child a certain experience (as of the Southwestern desert) that he can't repeat every day (living in the East in a town with lush vegetation in the summer), do you create something inside him (in the form of memory but also, perhaps, of unsatisfied desire) that he will want to return to the rest of his life?

The carton I happen to rest my feet on, under my desk, could also be con-sidered to contain a thick pile of thin sheets of memory—since each piece of paper (a miscellany thrown in there and not examined for years) or al-most each one yields a bit of memory or large piece of memory and along with the memory an emotion—a bit of emotion or a stronger emotion. But unexamined, it is (in the carton) all potential—like potential energy (the ball at the top of the incline, if I am remembering correctly) as opposed to kinetic energy as I studied this, with difficulty, in the very large, light-filled classroom up on a hilltop in Vermont, under the guidance of a physics and chemistry teacher whom I remember well, though he does not remember me. (And he said something about me at the time that I have kept in mind and returned to regularly all these years, and that helps to define me to myself, and yet he does not know who this woman in front of him is, and cannot even with all the help in the world revive any image of her as a girl.)

From all the sheets of paper—so thin as to be virtually two-dimen-sional—arise three-dimensional scenes visible only to me.

* * * * * * * * *

Speak, Memory by Nabokov in which the raw matter of his memory was developed and refined by the efflorescence of his language into more than it ever was in itself. He did not remember as much as he said. The memories grew in his language.

I go to the place, to Montaillou, for instance—and I am going "back" there, even though I have never been there before, because I have been there so often in imagination. I find only momentary, and tiny, traces of the past I am looking for. I find a treeless hillside with a cow path or sheep path worn on it, as so often imagined by me while I read the book I love, but at the next turn a development of modern "villas." There is no abundance, no richness, of remnants of the past but only remnants so nearly crowded out or extinguished by the present, by constructions of the present, that they have no more life in them, or almost none; they are defeated and nearly dead.

A certain life force prevails that can be destroyed, extinguished, by encroachment. On a hillside not far from here, a small treeless cemetery outlined in stone, within an irregular rectangular stone wall, had kept its life force, its magic, until a car wash (a tasteful one) was built a little too close to it—not right up against it, but within the same purview. Magic gone. As though the cemetery was fatally "insulted." Degradation.

A thing can be killed by its very preservation. Killed by the care to preserve it. Interruption, forever, of its growth, its coming into being, its death, in other words its own and owned life cycle. Preservation implying that it has no life force of its own but needs outside help to remain in existence, to remain in the world (not "alive," though). So that even if a bit of preserved "forest" remains here, something very important to it has died: its own force of being, its own insistence, without help.

Similarly, that those pieces of stone or wall, labeled with hand-written labels as coming from this or that particular place along the tour, should remain in the cupboard or cabinet of the house, though the family no longer lives there but has donated the house to the university, rather than in a museum or other place of formal exhibit, allows them to keep their life: that there is no rope around them, that they are still resting in a place that was natural for them to lie in, at the top of the house, in a drawer, preserved carefully but only as the family would preserve them, not the museum, allows them to continue the natural cycle of their life.

There is an old woman in black, in long skirts, sitting in the sun in a doorway in a small hilltop village in France. You are almost embarrassed to see
her there as you pass the bottom of the street and look up at the sunny
housefronts, because she seems an imitation of an old woman in black in
a hilltop village; there are no more women like that now knitting in the
sun, as there were for hundreds of years, as well as women in black skirts
sweeping their front step, by now they have all been depicted and over-
depicted, memorialized, they do not really live any longer, and where did
this one come from?

Memories creating three-dimensional space—recent memories shallow
space, older memories deeper space, oldest memories deepest space—(and
there is White in most mysterious Africa). The mind like a house—or an
apartment, to a city dweller. In the house, there is attic and basement, in
the apartment there are the farthest—most remote—rooms, unsuspected,
around corners, etc., always another where you thought the apartment
ended: this a recurring dream for years, I thought from my (real) frustration wanting at last an apartment large enough, now (the dream still recurring) having a house but wanting a larger house large enough, at last,
but "large enough" I realize now meaning containing rooms that stay
empty, that are not used and not even furnished; but perhaps all this time
that dream not reflecting any reality but only symbolizing the mind, the
mind needing another room and yet another, rooms scarcely known,
rooms mostly empty, filled mostly as yet with light and air and some dust
(dust being their own sign of a naturally continuing life, a too-clean room
having its own natural life interrupted).

The apartment has depth on a single level, horizontally (two-dimen-
sional), while the house has depth vertically (three-dimensional). The
mind in fact more like the apartment because I am reaching out for things
horizontally.

"Remember the Van Wagenens." Father's memory is mostly gone. Mother
is still alive, with a good memory, but some day, only my brother, besides
me, will know what this phrase means.

The Van Wagenens lived below us in that apartment building. We
stamped and stomped, and were reminded that we were not alone in the
building. I want to say to someone else, now, when he stamps and stomps,
"Remember the Van Wagenens!" and I am sad that he won't understand.
But why am I sad? Why do I want him to know about the Van Wagenens?

. . . .

And why couldn't I say, "Remember the Blacks" or, "Remember the Smiths" and give it the same meaning? Say that the Blacks or Smiths were our neighbors downstairs. Only Stephen, eventually, would know I was not telling the truth. But why does the truth matter?

When we did not stomp, but only shouted, we were reminded to remember the old woman next door; in an earlier building, it was the old couple next door. Now I have forgotten their names. Stephen will probably remember. He does not discover new memories, but he also does not forget old ones.

On television, someone says, approximately (I do not remember the exact words), "As we grow older, we can't help believing that the dead live on, in some way." This was in E. M. Forster's *Passage to India* in movie form, though it has taken me a moment to remember that.

see
88, 89

Odorous early morning fogs—in Graz or in Nottingham. I experience something like it today, or rather the two elements separately but simultaneously—mist in the hills out the window of the bus and at the same time a smell of some sort of fuel burning—and there is a deep physical desire in me to leap back into that fog, especially the fog of the Austrian early morning streets with trolley tracks in them. Wanting to go back into that past and into the past more generally why? Because it is not full of the unknown, as the future is, or because it is richer, sensually richer, as each succeeding year, in these times, in this country anyway, becomes poorer, sensually: more uniformity (less variety); cleaner people (fewer smells); more plastic surgery and better health (fewer physical deformities and "imperfections"); more television (less singing, dancing, playing on musical instruments, storytelling, cooking, gossiping); more "conveniences" (less labor of certain kinds, including cooking with its smells and tastes); more uniformity of speech (less dialect, less eccentricity of thought and behavior, fewer family expressions); more paving and construction (less wildlife, less wilderness, less vegetation); fewer kitchen gardens (neater properties, more clipping and cutting, less planting and growing); less backyard raising of poultry (fewer stinks and squawks, less mud).

Memory as distortion—I read something and remember it slightly wrong because what it actually said suggested a certain thought, somewhat related but not the same, something I wanted it to say, something I had been thinking, or wanted to think.

Then there is the memory of a thought or sequence of thoughts: walking by here two weeks ago this thought unfolded—moderately interesting at the time (kept me mildly entertained or occupied for the twenty seconds it took to unfold as I walked past this building), but not interesting at all now the second time; there is nothing left to do with it. Walking by here again now, as the same sequence begins its procession, I forcibly stop it. The most interesting thoughts (or thoughts that continue to be interesting) turn out to be the tricky problems that are not solved after only one or two ruminations (why did Layman P'ang put his head on the knee of his disciple when it came time for him to die?). (Another puzzle: the case of the man I read about in the newspaper who took a vow not to speak on Sundays—the fact that his perceptions were so much clearer. Was this because his "self" did not get in the way of his perceptions? Our speech so often bringing our intruding selves into the scene. *Open Mouth Already a Mistake.* A wonderful title, enjoyed over and over again—but also a good book, and also a good thing to remember.)

What was misheard, at a meeting: "breadth and depth" misheard as another pair of contrasts or contrasting dimensions: "breath and death." But the question is: when we do not mishear, when we *correctly* understand, do we not still hear the other words at the same time, though we may not consciously acknowledge this?

Memory: when you have a chance to compare, as you don't always, or very often, what you remember with the actual thing itself, there are almost always differences, some vast, some small: the very distinctly visualized page of that grammar book, with the lovely simple illustration at the top and the paragraph of simple narrative text below, and then below that the lovely simple double list of vocabulary, including, in the first lesson, *pupitre, cahier,* and *crayon,* is not after all quite the same as the actual page of the actual grammar book when I finally see it. Close, but not exactly the same, as Mlle Roser's face and figure are close but not exactly the same. (As our memory of a sentence of something read—so important to us that we refer to it in our own thinking quite often—may be close but not the same as the actual sentence, and sometimes crucially different, not the same thought at all.) And this necessarily means that we live closeted with, hedged in by, hosts and scores, sequences, chains, lines of memories all inaccurate.

We are excited by the stone—the shard from Hadrian's Wall—that we carry away in our pocket. As though we need physical proof that something happened. Otherwise, history told in the past tense may seem like a tall tale told in the past tense also, just as the tall tale told in the past tense pretends to be true, fact, history. For "true" history, we have the stories of historians, many accounts slightly different, maybe and maybe not true. Then we have what we are told are stones from Hadrian's Wall. We are excited, even if we never cared about Hadrian or his Wall. We are excited that many different things happened on this same spot of ground, layers of stories overlapping and covering the many spots of the one earth. As though, again, the past were a space that we could go back into. The past another space, one to enter to get away from this present.

One stands before the rubble of Hadrian's Wall imagining what occurred and unfolded when the wall still stood, and imagining what has occurred since. For that one, the air is thick with forms, colors. But to the one standing five feet behind the one imagining, to the one who does not know that these stones have any historical significance, the air is clear, the stones are only stones. All that activity is in the force of the imagining of the one five feet in front of him.

I do not know where Hadrian's Wall is, or if it still exists in any form. It is just a name that springs into my mind. I cannot even remember who Hadrian was, exactly.

The stones, the grammar book, the official document, the personal letter, the voice of a person who had been "lost" ("lost" as in the alumnae-magazine listings of "lost" alumnae, as for instance the early friend White): when we bring them in front of us, they suddenly have a present presence—they belong to the present, have a life in the present alongside their life in the past. Is that why we want to find them? To give them a life in the present to make their life in the past more real?

Sometimes I can't bear it that someone like Mlle Roser isn't still here—and this force of desire is what brings her back into the present in some other way, as: her life story written now, in the present, as I would like to write it; or as: a strong imagining that she still has consciousness in some form (with a willful disregard on my part of actual fact or possibility). The *not being able to bear it* is the *missing*. You want everything you want to be present all the time. What do we do about all these missing pieces?

Who is the woman talking to, who sits by her husband's grave and

talks to him? She is not "pretending" to talk to him. She is "really" talking to him. She is really talking to someone who is not there, or does not
seem to anyone but her to be there. Because of the force of her imagining.

In the brain cells, the old reality coexists with the new reality (the old reality being the training of memory, what memory, consistent over a long
time, has trained into those brain cells). For example, the new reality is
this feeble old man who doesn't know where his mouth is when he puts up
his hand to eat, but the old reality is still there in this old woman's brain
cells, so that in time of stress, exhaustion, and confusion (having fallen in
the dark in the middle of the night on her way to the bathroom, sick to her
stomach) she calls out: "Robert! Robert!" as though he would come help
her from his bed in the next room, and were not half a mile away in the
nursing home. And the old reality probably continues to be engraved on
brain cells that do not die, but are simply now accessible by routes different from the ones we use in waking, commonsensical life, accessible by
routes that become smooth and easy in sleep, exhaustion, panic, when we
are less "in control." And so, our childishness, at times of emotional
stress, may be simply the brain bypassing the more adult, controlled, later-
learned behavior, opening pathways to earlier reactions that are still engraved in us, not erased.

I see that I speculate, but do not want to go and read. I do not want to
go and find out how the brain "really" works, according to someone who
"knows." Maybe I don't want to admit that someone else may know
more about "my" brain than I do.

Oh, yes, though. I do believe everything has to be physical, all our emotions, even our "spiritual" life. What else can it be but physical?

Those vast apartments of the dreams—whatever they may symbolize, exactly (their symbolic character being just as "real" as their nonsymbolic
character), whether it is in fact the mind, in which case the mind dreams of
the mind, or something else—may be so often dreamt that now they are
present in waking life too, their presence felt constantly. Another place
(like the past) to go in the imagination: cease to see what is in front of us,
bulletin board or window filled with traffic, and now see that apartment,
spacious as we always desired so greatly but never had, or pasture with
cow path leading up to Alpine higher pasture that feels to be essential to
us, though exactly why? In what way essential?

. . . .

This woman reports to me what I had reported to her once, many years ago, and then forgotten: in the south of France, men who worked all day in the lavender fields would gather in the evenings in the bars, smelling of lavender. This was "my" piece of information, but I forgot it, and she remembered it, all these years. After she tells it to me now, I seem to remember it, it seems familiar. Had it been engraved in my mind also, but in a place where I did not have any access to it until now? Am I recalling it now, or learning it afresh? How can I tell?

I think that Mother is flirting with a man from her past who is not Father. But this is another example of the "old reality" coexisting alongside the "new reality." I say to myself: Mother ought to take care not to have improper contacts with this man "Franz"! (Franz who appeared in her life decades ago: she says, "I was the first American woman he had ever met.") Reaction of mine that comes bobbing up to the surface immediately: She should not see this man in an improper way while Father is "away"! But Father no longer lives at home; he now resides at Vernon Hall. I am also "forgetting" that my mother herself is ninety-four years old. There can be no improper relations with a woman of ninety-four, surely. Yet I suppose part of the confusion is that her capacity for subversion and betrayal is quite young and fresh, if her body is not.

In the pharmacy, family-owned, with a good steady stream of customers, several of whom are now waiting by the counter holding a prescription or some things they are about to buy, an old Englishman in a cream-colored zippered cardigan with remarkably frayed elbows, a scarf at the neck (perhaps an ascot), long silky white hair, an ear plug (or hearing aid), thick glasses, etc., looks up and straightens up over and over from writing a check in a large ledger on the counter to reminisce to a chance encounter about his service in South Africa piloting a plane during the war. His daughter or granddaughter, behind him and to one side holding his "stick," smiles. "He's ninety-two," she says, quietly, eventually. "He remembers everything." She radiates generosity, and unambivalent love. She does not try to hurry him along even gently, she is not worried that he keeps some customers waiting by the counter.

Maybe what she said was, "He does not forget anything."

I want to remember exactly what she said, but someone reading does not mind if it is not exact: Please, says that someone, just choose one or the other and get on with the story. Give me fiction—the approximation. Not the truth, with your doubt along with it.

You have no separable *memory* of having learned that word, but you understand that word or at least have a better sense of it than you could if you hadn't learned it at some point.

You pass a house in a strange town and it gives you a peculiar feeling—you know that something about it touches some memory and although you don't have access to the memory, the feeling comes to you, sometimes lightly, sometimes heavily. Houses in your own town, too familiar to you, may not trigger this same feeling because they are not fresh: the fresh house belongs to a certain type of house that triggers this feeling but it is a fresh example because it has a color, setting, ornamentation, light, etc., that you have not seen before.

And then: what about houses or other objects that do not explicitly call up a feeling: can it be that just under the surface a memory and a feeling are touched and influence your mood in a way beyond your grasp?

What about the "stimulating" effect of travel? Does travel provide not only a succession of new images and thoughts, but also a stream of fresh reawakenings of liminal or subliminal memories and feelings?

You see a paper case of arranged sewing and mending needles—anywhere, in a store, in your own workbasket—and *every time* this gives you a peculiar feeling. *What is it about those needles? What happened, all those many years ago?* You think it must have been in that sunny back bedroom where the old sewing machine was, with its wooden hood, and where you think sewing and mending went on. But did something happen, or was it just that you, a child, were suddenly struck by the beauty of those arranged needles?

The days' stimuli produce dreams that are either remembered or not remembered. If not remembered, then they are a part of our life in which we are actors but unaware of our actions, the "lost night" like the "lost weekend," night after night "lost."

But if you have nurtured, deep in your mind, an equivalency between house and mind or head, eyes and windows, when you look at house after

. . . .

house are you always, at another level, a less accessible level, seeing mind after mind, or head after head, eyes all around, on either side of the street?

The mind's inevitable habit of making metaphors: in Chinese calligraphy, "tiger" + "pig" = "wild boar." When we come upon an unfamiliar thing, we compare it to something familiar (book reviewers do this).

And possibly all elements of landscape affect us all the time metaphorically as well as really: he wants to live by water not only because of its real beauties—space, light, reflection, color, constant change and motion—but also its positive metaphorical properties, whatever they may be to him—cradling, nurturing, supporting?—whereas she is afraid of living by water because of its negative metaphorical associations for her: submersion, suffocation, the fact of being overwhelmed by a vastly greater presence than herself. She is more comfortable in a high place: a slight rise or prominence is good, a good place to put a house, for instance; but a mountaintop, even Alpine, is what she craves to experience at least periodically, not just for its real beneficial properties—fine view, good muscular ache in the legs getting up there, good cleansing of the lungs getting up there—but for its metaphorical properties: being "on top of" things, not letting things "get her down," having a "broad outlook," and a "sense of perspective." She cringes away from cramped valleys, narrow declivities, and craves the security of a high place, especially one bare of trees, open, preferably with meadows—and a cow or two or a few goats would not be unwelcome, the meadows being tamed or domesticated by the presence of assenting cows or goats (judgments of animals being reassuring, if often made in ignorance of the facts beyond their comprehension).

But is the craving for the Alpine meadow also conditioned or developed by early experiences that laid down a deposit of memories that in turn continue to affect development? (Though this is perhaps beside the point, experiences of sheer beauty may train a child to a certain appreciation of beauty.)

The child is taken to a mountain. Because there is already something in the child that craves a high place (up and well away from the submersive presence), this experience of the mountain is doubly moving and satisfying to the child. Then, the memory of that doubly satisfying experience of the mountain is added to the need that has always been present for what the mountain offers metaphorically, reinforcing the compelling pull of the mountain.

Do chronic mountain climbers always resume this quest for what the mountain offers really and metaphorically? As certain writers always write the same stories, or the same poems? As though certain things can be visited over and over but never quite said in such a way that they are over and done with? The mountain has been climbed, but it is still there.

Another possibility concerning what it means to climb a mountain: when so many difficulties in our lives seem mountainous, it is satisfying to climb an actual mountain. Unlike a difficulty, the mountain is not just *like* a mountain, it *is* a mountain; and it is also easier to climb, or at least simpler.

The Poetics of Space by Gaston Bachelard (though the translation could be improved, so that it would not seem so strange and difficult in places), and *Metaphors We Live By* by Lakoff and Johnson (though it doesn't go far enough or have enough in it).

Mrs. Palfrey at the Claremont by Elizabeth Taylor: reading this is a retreat into a depiction of an earlier reality—England in the 1960s in this case, but a very old-fashioned corner of it—and it is comforting because it is earlier, it is England, it was once real, England and English life were once reassuring—and if you grant that earlier ("past") realities have the same power as present ones, you feel you can choose to be elsewhere for a time and you will feel safe from this destructive present.

Curiously, when I actually lived in England in the 1960s, I was not in the least comforted or reassured. If, however, living there then, I had read a novel about England in the 1940s, I probably would have been comforted and reassured.

If stress or an excess or deficiency of certain chemicals changes the pathways in your brain, and you believe in the past reality and not the present one, or believe in your own created version of the present one, you really will be safe from this destructive present, since this present is pervasively destructive not so much physically, though it is destructive to much and to many physically, as psychically, to humans anyway.

I turn on the television in the middle of a difficult day, for distraction, and happen to encounter the same movie again, and watch it for a few minutes, and soon, though in a setting different from the one I had remembered, the words are spoken that I had been so surprised and glad to hear because I had been thinking the same thing, though they are not quite the

·   ·   ·   ·   ·   ·   ·   ·   ·   ·

words I had remembered. They are (preserved correctly because I wrote them down immediately):

"It's difficult, as we get older, not to believe that the dead live again."

What I had remembered, though still a double negative—"As we grow older, we can't help believing that the dead live on, in some way"—was a more positive double negative than what was actually said. In memory, I had altered the statement in a couple of ways to bring it closer to what I wished to believe myself.

Marketing Memory

. . . .

by

BERNARD COOPER

A few months before my third book, *Truth Serum*, was published, I lived in an emotional state familiar to many writers who are about to see their words in print: a phase of intense but not unbearable anticipation, a sense that one's work is teetering over the arena of public judgment—and is about to drop, unstoppable. Friends bolstered me with the analogy that one's book was like an offspring embarking on adulthood; all I could do now, they said, was watch from a doorway and wave good-bye. For a while, I was able to relinquish control of the book with some semblance of dignity and calm, but more and more often I found myself lapsing into an anxiety so extreme, I had to resist the temptation to phone my editor and offer to return my advance, with interest. The closer the publication date, the more vulnerable I felt. I began to suspect that my fraying courage, my growing dread of exposure, was in large part due to the fact that *Truth Serum*, unlike my first two books, was a memoir about my lifelong reckoning with homosexuality.

It may seem absurdly naive of me not to have understood, until so late, that a public probing of my personal life would be inevitable; after all, I had written in a genre which, rightly or wrongly, carries the promise of gossip and revelation. Interviewers would feel compelled, even invited, to ask impertinent questions, and reviews would of necessity touch upon the book's core subjects: my romantic relationship with a woman who became a lesbian; my psychiatrist's attempt to cure me of homosexuality with injections of sodium pentothol; my being the HIV-negative partner in a "sero-different" couple. Scant attention for the book, a prospect I'd earlier viewed as an indication of failure, now seemed like a potential blessing, and when other writers trotted out the old adage about negative criticism being better than none, I nursed a secret, self-defeating hope that, once out in the world, my book would be as innocuous as a polar bear in a snowstorm.

Of course, in the three years it took to write the book, I had deliberately explored personal subject matter. But a good memoir does more than dredge up secrets from the writer's past. A good memoir filters a life through resonant narrative, and in doing so must achieve a balance between language and candor. It was not the subject matter of my memoirs that I hoped would be startling, but rather language's capacity to name what was once nameless, to define what had once been vague and chaotic. The chief privilege of writing a memoir was the opportunity to go back and make sense of events that left me dumbstruck, mired in confusion, unarmed with the luminous power of words. Not until the book was on the verge of publication, however, did I fear that this gambit might be treated as a matter of exhibitionism rather than an aesthetic strategy. I'd purposely chosen intimate subjects, not in order to make them public, but because they drove me to probe more deeply the hidden meaning, imagery, and metaphors embedded in memory.

The first intrusion into my prepublication vacuum came in the form of a phone call, and it bore out my worst fears. A journalist wanted to ask me a few questions for an article he was writing on the preponderance of memoirs about to flood the bookstores. My publicist had warned me that the man felt a great deal of ambivalence about the memoir's current popularity, and was intent on challenging its legitimacy as a literary form. Still, she thought a mention in *Vogue* magazine was worth what she predicted would be a brief conversation. Two hours after he had called, the journalist, a former book reviewer for the *Washington Post*, was still pleading with me to confirm his antimemoir stance. It seemed he had set out to take memoirs to task, but once he'd read a few and had spoken to their authors, he could find little about them that was categorically reprehensible. His conviction was fading and he needed someone's approval in order to sustain his journalistic pluck.

"Don't you think there's a connection," he asked me, "between the popularity of talk shows and the popularity of memoirs?"

"Only if the author's motive in writing a memoir is to shock or lay blame or heal themselves by airing psychic damage. But there are different kinds of memoirs, just as their are different kinds of novels, and I don't

think it's fair to lump a tell-all in the same category with other, more literary works of autobiography."

"But don't you see the rise of the memoir as part of our culture's
narcissism?"

"People have been writing about themselves since the dawn of literature. Why can't a writer of prose bear witness to the particulars of his or
her life, as poets so often do?"

Our conversation took an unexpected psychotherapeutic turn when
Mr. S. confessed, without my prodding, that there was something about
memoirs that left him feeling "betrayed." By this time, his formerly busi-
nesslike voice had become agitated; he was going to vent his frustration no
matter how long it took. I feel compelled to mention that he kept me on
the telephone by offering pellets of occasional praise, assuring me that my
book was good, an exception to the rule. Although I was skeptical, it
worked like a charm, since even insincere praise produces in me a Pavlov-
ian surge of goodwill. "The problem," he told me, "is that I feel disappointed after reading a memoir because I've met a construct and not the
actual person."

"If you want to be *really* disappointed," I told him, "think how often
you meet a construct face-to-face. Or how often people you *think* you
know turn out to be constructs!"

"Yes, but there's a contract between reader and memoirist, an unstated
agreement that the writer is telling you the truth."

"Well, Mr. S., I read that contract, too, and I thought it only obligated
me to tell *my* version of the truth."

"At least in your book you occasionally say things like, 'I don't remember exactly' or 'It seems to me in retrospect. . . .'"

I had never thought of equivocation as a virtue, but again, I take my
compliments where I can get them. "No intelligent reader really believes
that a writer's memory is infallible. Wouldn't the 'truth'"—I drew invisible quotes in the air, that postmodern tic—"wouldn't the 'truth' be as boring and shapeless as an unedited transcript? Memoirists have to sculpt
and manipulate the truth in order to make it coherent and vivid and per-
suasive. That's the paradox: Only through artifice can one be truthful. Besides, there's a difference between facts and truth, and I don't always rely
on the facts to get to the truth."

"But if you're going to distort or exaggerate at all, why wouldn't you
call it fiction?"

"But if you're honoring real people and actual events, why *would* you
call it fiction?"

. . . .

A moment of silence. I glanced at the clock, as I assume did he.

Like Mr. S., I too reserve a healthy dose of suspicion about trends in the arts, particularly when those trends are commodified, turned into aesthetic or ideological bandwagons. And in all fairness, Mr. S. was asking some intelligent questions about the hazy border between fact and fiction, about the writer's responsibility, about the nature of artifice. Still, if one dismissed any genre or art movement because it raised difficult and unanswerable questions, as the memoir did for him, there would be no art and literature, except on T-shirts and coffee mugs. It could even be argued that the better the art, the more difficult and unanswerable the questions it raises. Both Mr. S. and I entertained, in fact, many of the same aesthetic questions; the difference between us (it seems to me in retrospect), is that he was troubled by ambiguity, and I was stirred by it.

Next, he revealed his trepidation as a critic. "There were two other memoirs by gay writers I decided not to review in this article because both of them wrote about their partners' deaths from AIDS. Don't you think it would be wrong to criticize such books?"

"Wrong?"

"Wouldn't it be like criticizing a book on the Holocaust?"

"But there are hundreds of books on the Holocaust, some more powerful than others. The more important the subject, the more skill the writer should bring to bear, and the more a critic should care that the writer not trivialize or sentimentalize."

"OK. Say I criticized the piece in your book about your HIV-positive partner. Wouldn't that upset you?"

"Yes, it would upset me. But I'm not exempt from criticism because I wrote about someone who's close to me and whose health is in jeopardy."

For the remainder of what for both of us had been an exhausting conversation, he asked me a few routine questions about my previous books, particularly the novel of mine that had preceded *Truth Serum*, and was based, I informed him, on the death of my older brother from leukemia. When the conversation finally ended, I sensed in his voice the disappointment and betrayal he spoke of earlier; all our philosophical footwork, all our aesthetic sparring, hadn't won me over to his side.

■ ■ ■

My conversation with Mr. S. was a joy compared to my reaction to the prepublication reviews. The first, I'm happy to report, was a starred review in *Kirkus*, and not since kindergarten have five-pointed stars seemed like such radiant geometric marvels. When my agent read me the review, I remember that my shoulders, which for weeks had been arching toward my ears, fell gently earthward. The wait, I believed, was over, my worry vindicated by sweet hyperbole. I clung to the review's last line, which urged the widest possible readership because of *Truth Serum's* craftsmanship. The very next day, however, my agent called with the review from *Publishers Weekly*. My agent is a tactful soul, and it pained me to hear his stoic tone when duty forced him to pelt me with insults. This reviewer claimed that my book *might* be of interest to "gay professionals" (by which I thought he really meant "professional gays") but that its craftless rambles were an attempt to claim that life, "when played in a homosexual key, is somehow more heroic."

No review has ever made me so miserable. It was bad enough to be accused of homosexual chauvinism, but worse was my resulting defensiveness. Late at night, in the midst of a fitful sleep, my thoughts would boil down to something plaintive, childlike, primal: "He hates me because I'm a big sissy." It was like being catapulted back though the decades and reliving every assault on my soft, unguarded, newly forming self. My life, I realized in the pale light of dawn, was open to jibes and scrutiny from all quarters. And because that life went undisguised, any reproach about the book, regardless how timid, would feel like an attack against me.

I brooded over this review for weeks. Although I had no proof, I assumed the reviewer was a straight man because heterosexual males, as a group, are more likely to engage in what psychologists call "protest behavior"—making vociferous public distinctions between oneself and an ostracized "other." For all I knew, the reviewer could have been a woman or another gay man, but I needed a well-defined and admittedly convenient figure toward whom to aim my protestations, which consisted chiefly of insisting that I abhor any art that makes a claim for group superiority. An account of the secrecy and self-deceit that is part of queer experience may seem, to unsympathetic ears, like "special pleading," or so I had to remind myself over and over

During this period of relentless internal monologues, I received another phone call from Mr. S. "I've finished the article," he announced brightly.

I chose "Oh" from the menu of appropriate noises, but couldn't understand why he had called to tell me this.

"I felt I should warn you," he continued, "that although I say yours was one of the few memoirs I liked, I'm going to criticize you for not men-

. . . .

tioning the death of your brother. I didn't know you had a brother until you mentioned him in our phone conversation, and anyone reading *Truth Serum* would think that you were an only child." He cleared his throat. "Is that OK?"

No detonated inside my head, but I heard myself say, "You're the critic."

In fact, I had three brothers, all of whom died from various ailments, a sibling history that strains even my credulity. I'd written about the death of my brothers in two previous books, and had consciously chosen not to cover that ground again in *Truth Serum*. My brothers were much older than I (there was a fifteen-year difference between the youngest of my older brothers and myself) and they lived away from home for the bulk of my youth. Very early in the writing of *Truth Serum*, I knew that a book concerned with homosexual awakening would sooner or later deal with AIDS and the population of friends I've lost to the disease. I also suspected I would write about my HIV-positive partner, Brian. To be blunt, I decided to limit the body count in this book in order to prevent it from collapsing under the threat of death. For the most part, however, this decision was personal rather than literary: there is only so much loss I can stand to place at the center of the daily rumination that writing requires. Were it only possible to contain in a single book the vast, senseless matrix of these deaths, but what skills I have jam and sputter and, ultimately, fail in the face of it. Only when the infinite has edges am I capable of making art.

I did my best to convey this reasoning to Mr. S., sighing with such a mix of melancholy and exasperation that my dog Zack walked over and planted himself at my side, as if to offer a sedative of warm fur and steady breath. "Would anything I'm telling you," I asked mid-explanation, "make a difference?"

"Well, no," he said. "I've already handed in the article. But I did say something positive about your discretion. I mean, being gay is no big deal these days. But in *Secret Life*, for example, the writer Michael Ryan writes about having sex with his dog! You wouldn't do that . . . would you?"

When I looked down at Zack, he raised his brown eyes and thumped his tail in a most appealing way.

Soon after the book came out, my publisher sent me on a small book tour. After a reading, people would sometimes commend me for my "honesty" and "courage" in writing about sexuality. (An ironic compliment for someone who had faced the prospect of his book tour with all the backbone of a sponge.) I thanked these people, but tried to explain that I felt neither honest nor brave when I worked with personal subjects because the rigors of shaping sentences and paragraphs overwhelmed any sense that I was dealing with risky or revealing subject matter. In the end, my history became so much raw material to temper in the forge of craft. In fact, the very familiarity of autobiographical material freed me up to concentrate on the sensual and emotional effects of language (for me the most pleasurable part of writing) instead of on the invention of story. I'd never flattered myself that my personal history is more exceptional or fascinating than most, but rather have seen it as a readily accessible source from which to write. Since "honesty" in writing is so often artless and indulgent, and since mere audacity so often masquerades as "courage," I was actually a little bothered by the suggestion that these were the work's most notable qualities. I'd hoped that the formal aspects of my autobiographical writing—its structure, language, and juxtaposition of images—were what made it worthwhile.

This "aesthetic distance," I began to see, had lulled me into a state of illusory safety while the memoir was being written. An illusion reinforced by the fact that I inhabit the realm of the midlist writer, a no-man's-land of chronic modesty and lowered expectations. The possibility that my book would garner much attention seemed fairly remote. At most I thought that, since the surge of memoirs by American writers was a topic of debate among people in the book business, some stray interest might fall my way. But once the tour was underway, it surprised me how frequently I was called upon to be a spokesperson for the memoir in general, or for the gay memoir in particular. For the first time in my career, I was part of a trend, and I found myself struggling against the prevailing current more often than swimming with it. It has always been hard enough for me to act as an advocate for my square inch of literary territory, and suddenly people expected me to answer questions about the literary marketplace, about the motives of other memoirists, about the suicide rate among gay youth, or the societal ramifications of same-sex marriage—issues I could not pretend to address with any degree of expertise. In other words, people expected me to be a generalist because I employ the public medium of language, when in fact language has always brought me closer to the exception, the sui generis, the self in its nearly inexpressible complexity.

Toward the end of my book tour, I took part in a panel discussion on the memoir, and discovered that I was not the only writer subjected to baffling questions. After we six panelists briefly discussed our memoirs, the moderator announced that she would take questions from the audience. Hands waved like a field of wheat. For the next forty minutes we heard what amounted to a single inquiry: *Should I hire an attorney?* This question was usually preceded by the synopsis of a memoir-in-progress: the psychotic sister inducted into a cult in Honolulu; the computer hacker who tapped into the Pentagon; the parent guilty of moral trespasses that were passionately hinted at but never named. It began to seem as if we live in a country virtually erupting with prosecutable secrets. We panelists took turns balking at questions like: *What kind of disclosures constitute libel? What's the necessity of changing names if a book's subject is deceased? Does the statute of limitations really matter when it comes to a small-press book? How reliable are the inhouse lawyers that publishers hire to give manuscripts a legal reading?* It was like a bad dream in which I'd gone to participate in an informal literary talk but ended up taking the Bar exam.

In San Francisco, as had happened throughout the book tour, people periodically came up to me and inquired about Brian's health. I often couldn't tell, for a disorienting instant, if these were people I knew, or who knew Brian; perfect strangers possessed a vague familiarity *because* of their concern. This interest in the well-being of my beloved was heartening; it allowed me to believe my writing had been intimate and engaging enough to create allies in what has sometimes been for us an isolating despair. And yet, I was taken aback each time it happened, reminded anew how this potential connection with a reader is, in the writer's long hours of solitude and uncertainty, at most a fond hope.

Understandably, Brian was not at all prepared to hear from those who learned about his HIV status from my book. One night, in fact, he came home from work and told me that someone had rushed up to him on the street, arms outstretched, to say he'd read that Brian was "dying." In fact, Brian was quite robust, and it upset me to think that I'd unwittingly dragged him into a spectacle of public sympathy that was the price—some might say the punishment—of having written frankly about our relationship. Aesthetic concerns had blinded me to the repercussions of frankness; more than writing *about* our relationship, I felt I was writing *through* our relationship; I'd tried to trace the day-by-day reclamation of our erotic life after Brian's diagnosis, not in order to describe us as a couple, or to boast about our passion, but in order to examine desire, which is protean, adaptable, and enduring.

Before the book was published, Brian and I had discussed at length how he might feel when the book came out, to what degree he was willing to have himself discussed in interviews, and even whether it would be advisable to withhold his last name from the dedication page, a request I was glad to honor. And yet, last name or no, he too was struck by the downright surreality of my, of our, fleeting brush with literary celebrity. The burden of responsibility weighed heavily on me during the writing of that section—I had to convey Brian's extraordinary optimism without glossing over his fear and physical suffering—and I continued to maintain a protective stance toward him after it appeared in print. And yet, each time he described some disconcerting encounter with someone who'd read about him in *Truth Serum*, it was all I could do not to interrupt and ask—forgive my writer's undernourished ego!—whether the person had liked my book.

During the brief spate of readings and reviews, people began to materialize from my past. An Armenian girl from the second grade whose sprightly manner I'd wanted desperately to emulate, phoned to say that she'd recognized herself in one memoir (she's now a district court judge and mother of two) and was curious to know what I'd been up to for the last forty years. The flamboyant arts and crafts teacher from my junior high school thrust out a now age-spotted hand and introduced himself before a reading. These were impromptu, dreamlike reunions; it had been so long since I'd last seen these people, and I'd resuscitated their memory through such an effort of will, that it stunned me to realize they were real after all—the flesh-and-blood bases, and not the products, of my imagination.

It could be argued that people from a fiction writer's past are just as likely to appear out of the blue when a novel is published. But typically these people have not populated the book one is promoting. One's characters, a sane writer would be quick to agree, do not call with congratulations, or surprise you by showing up at a book signing, a little worn around the edges and eager to catch up on old times.

It can also be argued that the experience of having *any* book enter the world leaves the author open to unforeseen reactions, and to the discomfort those reactions might cause. And yet, no matter how fervently the memoirists believe they can distinguish themselves from the thing they've made, it's not an altogether autonomous product that's held beneath the magnifying glass of critical assessment—it is, in essence, the sum of one's life.

The process of writing a memoir is insular, ruminative, a mining of privacies; once published, however, the book becomes an act of extroversion, an advertisement to buy, a performance of self rather than its articulation. The gap between these two experiences—the creation of a memoir and the ramifications of having written one—is wide enough, it seems to me, to bewilder even the most poised and gregarious among us. "No one who writes an autobiography can possibly know what they're in for," said Geoffrey Wolff, "until that book comes out."

Of all the surprises, however, the greatest for me has been this: by writing a memoir I've refashioned my past. *Truth Serum* has virtually supplanted my memories, so that, when asked about my personal history, I conjure up some section of the book. After all that labor, after worrying every sentence into being, those passages are deeply rooted, closely known. Most scenes, in fact, are far more vivid than the inklings, speculations, and stabs at accuracy from which they originated. It's as if some distillate of memory flooded the pages and turned them sanguine, leaving all that isn't recalled in that book pale and anemic.

The Polish writer Bruno Schultz said, "Memory is a filament around which our sense of the world has crystallized." Memoirs too are like those filaments; dipped in the cloudy solution of the past, words gather and congeal into books, and those books assume a life more intricate and eerie than the writer could second-guess.

Other People's Secrets

. . . .

by

PATRICIA HAMPL

The river is still now. Nighttime, and I have come here to sit alone in the dark in the wooden boat under its canvas roof, to tally up, finally, those I have betrayed. Let me count the ways. Earlier, white herds of cloud, way up there and harmless, buffaloed across the sky. A beautiful day, and everyone, it seemed, was on the water.

But now the pleasure craft that tooled back and forth all day, plying the marina's no-wake zone, are gone. Only a flotilla of linked barges rides high and empty, headed downriver to Lock Number Two at Hastings, intent on the river's serious business. The massive lozenges look strangely sinister as they part the dark water. By day these barges seem benign—riverine trucks, floating grain or ore or gravel between Saint Paul and the great Elsewhere. But now they pass by spectrally, huge and soundless.

Spotlights from the county jail send wavering columns of moon-colored light across the water from that side of the river to the marina on this side. I once saw a woman, standing on the Wabasha Bridge, lean as far over the guardrail as she could, and blow kisses toward the jail while traffic rushed around her. I followed her gaze and saw a raised arm clad in a blue shirt, indistinct and ghostly, motioning back from a darkened window. The loyal body, reaching even beyond bars to keep its pledge.

The boat groans in its slip, the lines that hold it fast strain as they absorb the wake from the barges. Boat, dock, ropes rub companionably against each other, sending out contented squeaks and low, reassuring moans that sound as if they're saying exactly what they mean—*tethered, tethered.*

This is the location in-between, not solid land, not high seas. Just a boat bobbing under a covered slip, the old city of my life laid out before me—the cathedral where my parents were married, the great oxidized bulb of its dome looking like a Jules Verne spaceship landed on the highest hill of the Saint Paul bluffs; on the near shore of Raspberry Island, an elderly Hmong immigrant casting late into the night for carp poisoned by PCBs; and downtown, in the middle distance, the bronze statue of the homeboy, F. Scott Fitzgerald, a topcoat flung over his arm even in summer, all alone at this hour in Rice Park, across from the sane neoclassical gray of the public library where it all began for me. "You'll like this place," my mother said, holding my hand as we entered—impossible luck!—a building full of books.

Let's start with mother, then, first betrayal.

It was all right to be a writer. In fact, it was much too grand, a dizzy height far above the likes of us. "Have you thought about being a librarian instead, darling?" At least I should get my teaching certificate, "to fall back on," she said, as if teaching were a kind of fainting couch that would catch me when I swooned from writing. But I knew I mustn't take an education course of any kind. Some canny instinct told me it is dangerous to be too practical in this life. I read nineteenth-century novels and Romantic poetry for four years, and left the university unscathed by any skill, ready to begin what, already, I called "my work."

I knocked around a jumble of jobs for ten years, working on the copy desk of the Saint Paul newspaper, recording oral histories in nursing homes around town—Jewish, Catholic, Presbyterian. I edited a magazine for the local public radio station. I lived in a rural commune on nothing at all, eating spaghetti and parsley with others as poetry-besotted as I, squealing like the city girl I was when a field mouse scurried across the farmhouse floor. I went to graduate school for two years—two more years of reading poetry. A decade of this and that.

Then, when I was thirty-two, my first book was accepted for publication, a collection of poems. My mother was ecstatic. She wrote in her calendar for that June day—practically crowing—"First Book Accepted!!" as if she were signing a contract of her own, one which committed her to overseeing an imaginary multiple-book deal she had negotiated with the future on my behalf. She asked to see the manuscript out of sheer delight and pride. My first reader.

And here began my career of betrayal. The opening poem in the manuscript, called "Mother/Daughter Dance" was agreeably imagistic, the predictable struggle of the suffocated daughter and the protean mother padded with nicely opaque figurative language. No problem. Only at the end, rising to a crescendo of impacted meaning, had the poem, seemingly of its own volition, reached out of its complacent obscurity to filch a plain and serviceable fact—my mother's epilepsy. There it was, the grand mal seizure as the finishing touch, a personal fact that morphed into a symbol, opening the poem, I knew, wide, wide, wide.

"You cannot publish that poem," she said on the telephone, not, for once, my stage mother egging me on. The voice of the betrayed, I heard for the first time, is not sad. It is coldly outraged.

"Why not?" I said with brazen innocence.

Just who did I think I was?

A writer, of course. We get to do this—tell secrets and get away with it. It's called, in book reviews and graduate seminars, courage. *She displays remarkable courage in exploring the family's. . . . the book is sustained by his exemplary courage in revealing. . . .*

I am trying now to remember if I cared about her feelings at all. I know I did not approve of the secrecy in which for years she had wrapped the dark jewel of her condition. I did not feel she *deserved* to be so upset about something that should be seen in purely practical terms. I hated—feared, really—the freight she loaded on the idea of epilepsy, her belief that she would lose her job if anyone "found out," her baleful stories of people having to cross the border into Iowa to get married because "not so long ago" Minnesota refused to issue marriage licenses to epileptics. The idea of Iowa being "across the border" was itself absurd.

She had always said she was a feminist before there was feminism, but where was that buoyant *Our Bodies, Ourselves* spirit? Vanished. When it came to epilepsy, something darkly medieval had bewitched her, making it impossible to appeal to her usually wry common sense. I rebelled against her shivery horror of seizures, although her own had been successfully controlled by medication for years. It was all, as I told her, no big deal. Couldn't she see that?

Stony silence.

She was outraged by my betrayal. I was furious at her theatrical secrecy. Would you feel this way, I asked sensibly, if you had diabetes?

"This isn't diabetes," she said darkly, the rich unction of her shame refusing my hygienic approach.

Even as we faced off, I felt obscurely how thin my reasonableness was. The gravitas of her disgrace infuriated me partly because it had such natural force. I was a reed easily snapped in the fierce gale of her shame. I sensed obliquely that her loyalty to her secret bespoke a firmer grasp of the world than my poems could imagine. But poetry was everything! That I knew. Her ferocious secrecy made me feel foolish, a lightweight, but for no reason I could articulate. Perhaps I had, as yet, no secret of my own to guard, no humiliation against which I measured myself and the cruelly dispassionate world with its casual, intrusive gaze.

I tried, of course, to make *her* feel foolish. It was ridiculous, I said, to think anyone would fire her for a medical condition—especially her employer, a progressive liberal-arts college where she worked in the library. "You don't know people," she said, her dignified mistrust subtly trumping my credulous open-air policy.

This was tougher than I had expected. I changed tactics. Nobody even reads poetry, I assured her shamelessly. You have nothing to worry about.

She dismissed this pandering. "You have no right," she said simply.

It is pointless to claim your First Amendment rights with your mother. My arguments proved to be no argument at all, and she was impervious to any blandishment.

Then, when things looked lost, I was visited by a strange inspiration.

I simply reversed field. I told her that if she wanted, I would cut the poem from the book. I paused, let this magnanimous gesture sink in. "You think it over," I said. "I'll do whatever you want. But Mother . . ."

"What?" she asked, wary, full of misgivings as well she might have been.

"One thing," I said, the soul of an aluminum-siding salesman rising within me, "I just want you to know—before you make your decision—it really is the best poem in the book." Click.

This was not, after all, an inspiration. It was a gamble. And although it was largely unconscious, still, there was calculation to it. She loved to play the horses. And I was my mother's daughter; instinctively I put my money on a winner. The next morning she called and told me I could publish the poem. "It's a good poem," she said, echoing my own self-promoting point. Her voice was rinsed of outrage, a little weary but without resentment.

Describe it as I saw it then: she had read the poem, and like God in His heaven, she saw that it was good. I didn't pause to think she was doing me a favor, that she might be making a terrible sacrifice. This was good for her, I told myself with the satisfied righteousness of a nurse entering a terrified patient's room armed with long needles and body restraints. The wicked witch of secrecy had been vanquished. I hadn't simply won (although that was delicious). I had liberated my mother, unlocked her from the prison of the dank secret where she had been cruelly chained for so long.

I felt heroic in a low-grade literary sort of way. I understood that poetry—my poem!—had performed this liberating deed. My mother had been unable to speak. I had spoken for her. It had been hard for both of us. But this was the whole point of literature, its deepest good, this voicing of the unspoken, the forbidden. And look at the prize we won with our struggle—for doesn't the truth, as John, the beloved apostle promised, set you free?

■ ■ ■

Memory is such a cheat and privacy such a dodging chimera that between the two of them—literature's goalposts—the match is bound to turn into a brawl. Kafka's famous solution to the conundrum of personal and public rights—burn the papers!—lies, as his work does, at the conflicted heart of twentieth-century writing, drenched as it is in the testimony of personal memory and of political mayhem.

Max Brod, the friend entrusted to do the burning, was the first to make the point in his own defense, which has been taken up by others ever since: Aside from the unconscionable loss to the world if he had destroyed the letters and the journals with their stories and unfinished novels, Brod, as his good friend Kafka well knew, was a man incapable of burning a single syllable. Kafka asked someone to destroy his work whom he could be sure would never do so. No one seriously accuses Brod of betraying a dying friend. Or rather, no one wishes to think about the choice in ethical terms because who would wish he had lit the match?

But one person did obey. Dora Diamant, Kafka's final and certainly truest love, was also asked to destroy his papers. She burned what she could, without hesitation. She took Kafka at his word—and he was alive to see her fulfill his command. She was never wife or widow, and did not retain any rights over the matter after Kafka's death, but even Brod, Kafka's literary executor, felt it necessary to treat her diplomatically, as late as 1930, and to present his case to her when he set about publishing the work.

As she wrote to Brod during this period when they tried to come to an understanding about publication of Kafka's work:

> The world at large does not have to know about Franz. He is nobody else's business because, well, because nobody could possibly understand him. I

regarded it—and I think I still do so now—as wholly out of the question for anyone ever to understand Franz, or to get even an inkling of what he was about unless one knew him personally. All efforts to understand him were hopeless unless he himself made them possible by the look in his eyes or the touch of his hand. . . .

Hers is the austere, even haughty claim of privacy, a jealous right, perhaps. She knew it: "I am only now beginning to understand . . . the fear of having to share him with others." This, she freely admits to Brod, is "very petty." She does not claim that her willingness to destroy the work was a wholly noble act. She is surprisingly without moral posturing.

Still, she could not bear to give the world those works she had not destroyed. As Ernst Pawel says in *Nightmare of Reason: A Life of Franz Kafka*, she denied that she had them until after her marriage to a prominent German Communist when their house was raided by the Gestapo in 1933 and every piece of paper, including all the Kafka material, was confiscated, never to be located to this day. She was, finally, distraught, and as Pawel says, "confessed her folly" to Brod.

Pawel, an acute and sensitive reader of Kafka and his relationships, puzzles over this willful act of secrecy. "The sentiment or sentimentality that moved this otherwise recklessly truthful woman to persist in her lie," he writes, clearly perplexed, ". . . may somehow be touching, but it led to a tragic loss."

Yes—but. The lie Dora Diamont persisted in was a simple one—her refusal to admit to Kafka's editors or friends that she still possessed any of his papers. But her letter to Brod (written three years before the Gestapo raid) is not the document of a woman who is simply "sentimental." She is adamantly antiliterary. The papers she refused to hand over—and which, terrible irony, were swept away by the Gestapo into that other kind of silence, the wretched midcentury abyss—were, no doubt quite literally to her, private documents. After all, most of Kafka's works were written in—or as—journals. There is no more private kind of writing. The journal teeters on the edge of literature. It plays the game of having its cake and eating it too: writing which is not meant to be read.

The objects Kafka asked Dora Diamant to destroy and those she later refused to hand over to editors did not have the clear identity of "professional writing" or of "literature." They were works from a master of prose writing, but they were still journals and letters. They must have seemed, to the woman who had lived with them, intensely personal documents. If it is understood even between lovers that a journal is "private," off limits, not to be read, it doesn't seem quite so outrageous that Dora Diamant, who loved the man, would choose to honor his privacy as she did. In fact, it is not a mystery at all, but quite in keeping with her character as a "recklessly truthful woman."

Privacy and expression are two embattled religions. And while the god of privacy reigns in the vast air of silence, expression worships a divinity who is sovereign in the tabernacle of literature. Privacy, by definition, keeps its reasons to itself and can hardly be expected to borrow the weapons of expression—language and literature—to defend itself. To understand the impulse of privacy that persists against every assault, as Dora Diamant's did, her position must not call forth the condescension of seeing her adamant refusal as being merely "touching."

In her 1930 letter to Brod, Dora Diamant is trying to express what she maintains—against the institutional weight and historical force of literature—is a greater truth than the truth that exists in Kafka's papers. She is determined to remain loyal to his appalling absence and to the ineffable wonder of his being, "the look in his eyes," "the touch of his hand."

This is not sentimentality. She speaks from a harsh passion for accuracy—nothing but his very being is good enough to stand as his truth. Literature at best is a delusion. It is the intruder, the falsifier. She makes an even more radical claim—it is unnecessary: "The world at large does not have to know about Franz." Why? Because their "knowing" (possible only through the work now that he is dead) is doomed to be incomplete and therefore inaccurate. A lie, in other words. In her terms, it is a bigger lie, no doubt, than her refusal to admit to those eager editors that she did indeed have the goods stashed away in her apartment.

No writer could possibly agree with her. Except Kafka, of course. But maybe Kafka wasn't "a writer." It may be necessary to call him a prophet. In any case, Dora Diamant wasn't a writer. She belonged to the other religion, not the one of words, but the human one of intimacy, of hands that touch and eyes that look. The one that knows we die, and bears silently the grief of this extinction, refusing the vainglorious comfort of literature's claim of immortality, declining Shakespeare's offer:

> *So long as men can breathe or eyes can see,*
> *So long lives this, and this gives life to thee.*

The ancient religions all have injunctions against speaking the name of God. Truth, they know, rests in silence. As Dora Diamant, unarmed

. . . .

against the august priests of literature who surrounded her, also knew in her loneliness: what happens in the dark of human intimacy is holy, and belongs to silence. It is not, as we writers say, material.

■ ■ ■

There is no betrayal, as there is no love, like the first one. But then, I hadn't betrayed my mother—I had saved her. I freed her from silence, from secrecy, from the benighted attitudes that had caused her such anguish, and from the historical suppression of women's voices—and so on and so forth. If Dora Diamant was someone who didn't believe in literature, I was one who believed in nothing else.

This defining moment: I must have been about twelve, not older. A spring day, certainly in May because the windows, and even the heavy doors at Saint Luke's School are open. Fresh air is gusting through the building like a nimble thief, roller shades slapping against windows from the draft, classroom doors banging shut. The classrooms are festooned with flowers, mostly drooping masses of lilac stuck in coffee cans and mason jars, placed at the bare feet of the plaster Virgin who has a niche in every classroom: *Ave, ave, Ma-ree-ee-ah*, our Queen of the May.

For some reason we, our whole class, are standing in the corridor. We are waiting—to go into the auditorium, to go out on the playground, some everyday thing like that. We are formed in two lines and we are supposed to be silent. We are talking, of course, but in low murmurs, and Sister doesn't mind. She is smiling. Nothing is happening, nothing at all. We are just waiting for the next ordinary moment to blossom forth.

Out of this vacancy, I am struck by a blow: *I must commemorate all this*. I know it is just my mind, but it doesn't feel like a thought. It is a command. It feels odd, and it feels good, buoyant. Sister is there in her heavy black drapery, also the spring breeze rocketing down the dark corridor, and the classroom doorway we are standing by, where, inside, lilacs are shriveling at the bare feet of Mary. Or maybe it is a voice that strikes me, Tommy Howe hissing to—I forget to whom, "OK, OK, lemme go."

These things matter—Tommy's voice, Sister smiling in her black, the ricochet of the wind, the lilacs collapsing—because I am here to take them in.

That was all. It was everything.

I have asked myself many times about that oddly adult word—*commemorate*—which rainbows over the whole gauzy instant. I'm sure that was the word, that in fact this word was the whole galvanizing point of the experience because I remember thinking even at the time that it was a weird word for a child—me—to use. It was an elderly word, not mine. But I grabbed it and held on. Perhaps only a Catholic child of the 1950s would be at home with such a conception. We "commemorated" just about everything. The year was crosshatched with significance—saints' feast days, holy days, Lent with its Friday fasts and Stations of the Cross. We prayed for the dead, we prayed *to* the dead.

How alive it all was. Commemoration was the badge of living we pinned on all that happened. Our great pulsing religion didn't just hold us fast in its claws. It sent us coursing through the day, the week, the month and season, companioned by meaning. To honor the moment, living or dead, was what "to commemorate" meant. This, I sensed for the first time, was what writers did. Of course, being a Catholic girl, I was already sniffing for my vocation. Sister was smiling, her garments billowing with the spring wind, and here was "the call," secular perhaps, but surely a voice out of the whirlwind.

■ ■ ■

The sense of the fundamental goodness of the commemorative act made it difficult to believe "commemoration" could be harmful. Beyond this essential goodness I perceived in the act of writing, I felt what I was up to was a kind of radiance, a dazzling shining-forth of experience. I never liked the notion that writers "celebrated" life—that was a notion too close to boosterism and the covering-over of life I thought writers were expressly commissioned to examine. But who could be hurt by being honored—or simply noticed? Who could object to that?

A lot of people, it turned out. My mother was only the first. "You can use me," a friend once said, "just don't abuse me." But who, exactly, makes that distinction?

"You're not going to *use* this, are you?" someone else asked after confiding in me. She regarded me suddenly with horror, as if she had strayed into a remake of *Invasion of the Body Snatchers* where she played a real human who has just discovered I'm one of *them*.

Later, I strayed into a scary movie myself. I'd become friendly one year with a visiting writer from one of the small, indistinct countries "behind the Iron Curtain," as we used to say. It was a year of romantic upheaval for me—for her too. God knows what I told her. We met for coffee now

. . . .

and again, and regaled each other with wry stories from our absurdist lives. Then she went back where she had come from.

A year later I received in the mail a book in a language completely unknown to me. When I saw her name on the cover I realized this was the book she had been writing in Minnesota. "Just wanted you to have my little American book!" the cheery note said. An American publisher was interested in releasing an English translation, she added. I flipped through the incomprehensible pages. Suddenly, two hideous words cleared the alphabet soup with terrible eloquence: *Patricia Hampl.* Then I saw, with increasing alarm, that my name—me!—popped up like a ghoulish gargoyle throughout the text, doing, saying, I knew not what.

"I don't think you'll be too upset," someone who could read the incomprehensible language told me, but declined to translate. "It's a little sticky," she said vaguely. Sticky?

Later still, at a workshop with a Famous Novelist, I raised my hand and posed the question. "You've said in interviews that your fiction is autobiographical," I began, notebook ready to take down his good counsel. "I'm wondering what advice you might have on writing about family or close friends?"

"Fuck 'em," he said. And I shivered the body-snatcher shiver. So you *do* have to become one of them?

Over the years, as other books followed my first, I told the story of how I had spoken for my mother who could not speak for herself. I had all my ducks lined up in a row—my belief in the radiance of the commemorative act, my honorable willingness to let my mother decide the fate of the poem, her plucky decision to let me publish the poem, which at first she had seen as a cruel invasion but which—the real miracle—she came to recognize was nothing less than a liberation for her. She and I, together, had broken an evil silence. See what literature can do?

Then one day I got a call from a poet who was writing a piece about "personal writing." She had been in an audience where I had told my mother-daughter story. There had been many; by this time I had my patter down. It was a wonderful story, she said. Could she use it in her essay as an example of . . . ?

The words "wonderful story" hung above me like an accusation. The blah-blah-blah of it all came back and stood before me, too contemptuous even to slap me in the face. I felt abashed. I told her I wanted to check the story first with my mother.

She answered the phone on the first ring. She was still working, still at her library job. *Remember that poem in my first book*, I said, *the one that has the seizure in it and you and me?*

Oh yes.

Remember how I told you I wouldn't publish it if you didn't want me to, and you said I could go ahead?

Yes.

Well, I was just wondering. Is that something you're glad about? I mean, do you feel the poem sort of got things out in the open and sort of relieved your mind, or—I sounded like a nervous teenager, not the Visiting Writer who had edified dozens of writing workshops with this exemplary tale—*or . . .*

What *was* the or? What was the alternative?

Or did you just do it because you loved me?

Without pausing a beat: *Because I loved you.*

Then the pause: *I always hated it.*

■ ■ ■

Bobbing again on the water in the old boat, still in-between. A nightly ritual, but now, as if on cue for the climax, lightning has begun to knife the sky, and thunder has started its drumrolls. Hot summer night, waiting to break open the heat, and spill.

No wonder I like to come down here, to this floating place. I was attracted too to the in-between position of the writer. More exactly, I was after the suspended state that comes with the act of writing: not happy, not sad; uncertain of the next turn, yet not lost; here, but really *there*, the there of an unmapped geography which, nonetheless, was truly home—and paradisal.

The elusive pleasure to be found in writing (and only *in* it, not the *before* of anticipation, not the *after* of accomplishment) is in following the drift, inkling your way toward meaning. My old hero, Whitman, that rogue flaneur, knew all about it: "I am afoot with my vision!" he exulted. It was an *ars poetica* I too could sign up for, basking in the sublime congruence of consciousness "afoot" in the floating world.

There are, it is true, memoirists who are not magnetized by memory. They simply "have a story to tell." They have the goods on someone—mother, father, even themselves in an earlier life, or on history itself. "Something" has happened to them. These stories—of incest or abuse, of extraordinary accomplishment or exceptional hardship, the testimonies

· · · · · · · · · ·

of those who have witnessed the hellfire of history or the anguish of un-
usually trying childhoods—are what are sometimes thought of as the real
or best occasions of autobiography.

Memory, in this view, is a minion of experience. It has a tale to tell. Its
job is to witness the real or to reveal the hidden. Sometimes the impulse to
write these accounts is transparently self-serving or self-dramatizing. But
at least as often, and certainly more valiantly, this is the necessary literature of witness. Historic truth rests on such testimony. The authority of
these personal documents is so profound, so incriminating, that whole ar-
senals of hatred have been arrayed in mad argument for half a century in
a vain attempt to deny the truth of a little girl's diary. These kinds of memoir count for a lot. Sometimes they are the only history we can ever hope
to get.

Still, memory is not, fundamentally, a repository. If it were, no question
would arise about its accuracy, no argument would be fought over its no-
torious imprecision. The privacy of individual experience is not a right as
Dora Diamant tried to argue with Max Brod, or as my mother begged me
to see. Not a right, but something greater—it is an inevitability that returns no matter what invasion seems to overtake it. This privacy is bred of
memory's intimacy with the idiosyncrasy of the imagination. What memory "sees," it must regard through the image-making faculty of mind. The
parallel lines of memory and imagination cross finally, and collide in narrative. The casualty is the dead body of privacy lying smashed on the
track.

Strangely enough, contemporary memoir, all the rage today as it practically shoves the novel off the book-review pages, has its roots not in fiction, which it appears to mimic and tease, but in poetry. The chaotic lyric
impulse, not the smooth drive of plot, is the engine of memory. Flashes of
half-forgotten moments flare up from their recesses: the ember red tip of a
Marlboro at night on a dock, summer of 1954, the lake still as soup, or a
patch of a remembered song unhinged from its narrative moorings—
Glow little glow worm, glimmer, glimmer, and don't forget the skinned
knuckle—Dad's!—turning a dead ignition on a twenty-below winter day.
Shards glinting in the dust.

These are the materials of memoir, details that refuse to stay buried,
that demand habitation. Their spark of meaning spreads into a wildfire of
narrative. They may be domesticated into a story, but the passion that
begat them as images belongs to the wild night of poetry. It is the humble
detail, as that arch memorialist Nabokov understood, which commands

detail or
retrieval
cue

"Caress the detail, the
divine detail,"
Nabokov

memory to speak: "Caress the detail," he advised, "the divine detail."
And in so doing, he implicitly suggested, the world—the one lost forever—
comes streaming back. Alive, ghostly real.

Kafka called himself "a memory come alive." His fellow townsman,
Rilke, also believed that memory, not "experience," claims the sovereign
position in the imagination. How strange that Kafka and Rilke, these two
giants who preside as the hieratic figures, respectively, of The Writer and
The Poet for the modern age, were both Prague boys, born barely eight
years apart, timid sons of rigid fathers, believers in the word, prophets of
the catastrophe that was to swallow their world whole, and change literature forever. Canaries sent down into the mine of history, singing till the
end.

In *Letters to a Young Poet*, the little book it is probably safe to say
every young poet reads at some point, Rilke wrote to a boy who was a student at the very military academy where he himself had been so notori-
ously miserable. He wrote, no doubt, to his younger self as well as to this
otherwise unknown student poet Franz Zaver Kappus. Although the boy
was only nineteen, Rilke sent him not forward into experience, but deeply
inward to memory as the greatest "treasure" available to a writer.

"Even if you found yourself in some prison," Rilke says in the first letter, "whose walls let in none of the world's sounds—wouldn't you still
have your childhood, that jewel beyond all price, that treasure house of
memories?"

This is not an invitation to nostalgia—Rilke had been painfully unhappy as a boy, stifled and frightened. He was not a sentimentalist of
childhood. He is directing the young poet, rather, to the old religion of
commemoration in whose rituals the glory of consciousness presides. He
believes, as I cannot help believing as well, in the communion of perception where experience does not fade to a deathly pale, but lives evergreen,
the imagination taking on the lost life, even a whole world, bringing it
to the only place it can live again, reviving it in the pools and freshets of
language.

■ ■ ■

I have gone to visit my mother. She is in the hospital, has been there now
many weeks. "It's hell to get old," she says, barely voiced words escaping
from the trach tube from which she breathes. Almost blind, but still eager
to get back to her e-mail at home. She smiles from her great charm, a be-

. . . .

atific smile, when I say "e-mail," when I say "home." There is a feeding tube in her stomach. There was a stroke, then her old nemesis, a seizure, a heart attack, respiratory this, pulmonary that—all the things that can go wrong, all the things that have their high-tech solutions. She is surrounded by beeps and gurgles, hums and hisses. She'll get home. She's a fighter. At the moment, fighting her way out of the thick ether of weeks of sedative medicines.

She is glad I have come. She has been, she tells me, in a coffin at Will-wersheid's Mortuary. Terrible experience, very confining.

I tell her she has not been in a coffin, I assure her she has not been at a funeral parlor. I tell her the name of the hospital where she is.

She looks at me as at a fool, not bothering to conceal her contempt. Then the astonishing firmness that kept me in line for years: *I have been in a coffin. Don't tell me I have not been in a coffin.*

Well, I say, you're not in a coffin now, are you?

No, she says, agreeing with vast relief, *thank God for that.*

The trip, she says animatedly, trying to express the marvel of it all, has been simply *amazing.* Shipboard life is wonderful. Skirting Cuba—that was beautiful. But the best part? The most beautiful, wonderful black woman—a real lady—came to her cabin with fresh linens. The ironing smelled so good! That was what made Port au Prince especially nice. People everywhere, she says, have been so lovely.

Why not? It's better than the coffin at Willwersheid's. Then, the air, saturated by weeks of medication, suddenly clears, and we're talking sensibly about people we know, about politics—she knows who's running for governor, and she wouldn't vote for Norm Coleman if he were the last man on earth. We see eye-to-eye. She asks about my father, she asks about my work—our usual subjects.

"Actually," I say, "I'm writing about you. Sort of."

She's in a wheelchair, the portable oxygen strapped to the back. We have wheeled down to the visitors' lounge and are looking out the big picture window that has a view of the capitol building and the cathedral, and even a slender curve of the Mississippi in the distance where I will go when I leave here, to sit again to brood in the little boat under the canvas slip. She can make out the capitol and the cathedral. Storms grizzle the sky with lightning, and her good eye widens with interest.

I say I am trying to tell the story again of the poem about the seizure. "I'm trying to explain it from your point of view," I say.

She nods, takes this in. "Yes," she says slowly, thoughtfully. "That's

good you're doing that finally. It's very important to . . . to my career."
Her smile, the great rainbow that the nurses have remarked on, beams in
my direction, the wild sky behind us, flashing.

Her career. Yes. Her own passage through this life, the shape she too
has made of things, her visions, the things she alone knows. The terrible
narrowness of a coffin and the marvels of Port au Prince, the astonishing
kindness of people, the pleasure of sweet-smelling linen. I can see now that
she was standing up for the truth of her experience, the literal fact of it,
how it jerked and twisted not only her body but her life, how it truly
seized her. My poem and I—we merely fingered the thing, casually displaying it for the idle passerby. What she knows and how she knows it
must not be taken from her.

I never understood the fury my desire to commemorate brought down
upon me. The sense of betrayal—when I thought I was just saying what I
saw, drawn into utterance, I truly believed, by the buoyancy of loving life,
all its strange particles. I didn't have a dark story of abuse to purvey or
even a horde of delicious gossip. I was just taking pictures, I thought. But
then, doesn't the "primitive" instinct know that the camera steals the
soul? My own name skittering down the pages of a foreign book, sending
alarms down my spine. The truth is: to be written about feels creepy. The
constraining suit of words rarely fits. Writers—and readers—believe in the
fiction of telling a true story. But the living subject knows it as the work of
a culprit.

Years ago, when I was living in the poetry commune, eating spaghetti
and parsley, I had a dream I knew would stay with me. A keeper, as my father says of fish. I was behind the wheel of a Buick, a big improbable Dad
car I couldn't imagine driving in real life. I was steering with my eyes shut,
traveling the streets of my girlhood—Linwood, Lexington, Oxford, even
Snelling with its whizzing truck traffic. It was terrifying. I understood I
must not open my eyes. And I must not turn the wheel over to the man sitting beside me in the passenger seat although he had his eyes wide open. If
I wanted to reach my destination (murky, undefined), I must keep driving
blind. My companion kept screaming, "You'll kill us all!"

I've lost a quite a few people along the way. And not to death. I lose
them to writing. The one who accused me of appropriating her life, the
one who said he was appalled, the poet miffed by my description of his
shoes, the dear elderly priest who said he thought I understood the meaning of a private conversation, this one, that one. Gone, gone. Their fading

. . . .

faces haven't faded at all, just receded, turned abruptly away from me, as is their right.

I have the letters somewhere, stuffed in a file drawer I never open. The long letters, trying to give me a chance to explain myself, the terse ones, cutting me off for good. The range of tone it is possible for the betrayed to employ—the outrage, the disgust, the wounded astonishment, the quiet dismay, the cold dismissal. Some of them close friends, some barely known, only encountered. All of them "used," one way or another, except for the baffling case of the one who wrote to complain because I had *not* included her.

Mother and I are safe inside, staring out the big hospital window as our city gets lost in sheets of gray. "Is it raining?" she asks. The storm is a wild one, bending old trees on Summit Avenue, snapping them easily, taking up clots of sod as they go down. At the river the boat must be banging against the dock.

My mind scrolls up again the furious swirl of repeating phrases in those letters from people who no longer speak to me. And me, surprised every time. *I cannot believe that you would think . . . Maybe it seemed that way to you, but I . . .*

But I'm getting too close again, hovering at their sides where they don't want me, trying to take down the dialogue. Better not. Leave the letters in their proud silence. No quotes, no names. Or else, someone, in a dream or elsewhere, is likely to rise up in fury, charging with the oracular voice of the righteous dead that I've killed again.

*What makes a good story?
what makes a good explanation?
A good explanation is a story your
grandmother could understand;
when you write your essay, "tell me
a story" — set it up
so that it "works" in the
way a story "works"*

Tell Me a Story

*kind of complexity
puzzle . . . .
problem
story*

by

MICHAEL RYAN

When I was little boy, my father told me bedtime stories about the Greenies. The Greenies were a race of tiny people—three feet tall—who lived inside the earth. My father had discovered them when he was my age exploring caves in the Ozarks where he grew up on a dirt farm. He'd entertain himself climbing deep down in the dark, among bats and stalagmites and stalactites, further down than anyone had ever gone. One day, he saw an odd light coming through a crack above a ledge high up in the cave wall, almost hidden by rocks. He climbed up and by moving the rocks he saw an opening just large enough for him to squeeze through. There was a ledge on the other side, too, and there in the great cavern beneath him, in a shining city made of emeralds, diamonds, platinum, and gold, he saw the Greenies, all scurrying this way and that like ants. It was terrifically hot and damp, the stones around him radiated heat. When he climbed down closer he could see their pale green skin tough as rhinoceros hide and their corkscrew-tipped heads that could drill through granite. There was a good Greenie king, a gorgeous Greenie princess who was in love with my father (gorgeous, I guess, despite her corkscrew-tipped head), bad Greenies who had left the city and threatened it with raids, and assorted natural cataclysms and fantastic monsters.

The detail I remember best was incidental to the big battles and epic struggle for racial survival. After my father had helped the Greenies and been accepted and honored by them, he was given full access to their kingdom, permission never before granted to an outsider. He could roam about wherever he wanted and treat whatever they had as his own—the latter privilege he didn't exercise except for the three modest, perfect diamonds he took for his mother, for the woman he would someday marry (this diamond could be found in my mother's engagement ring), and for himself (here was his, in the gold ring on his right hand; he said someday, when he was dead, it would be mine). One quiet day in the kingdom, happy and content with these harmonious, gentle people, he was exploring its outer reaches by himself and, in a grotto on the other side of a stream, he came upon a goat with a head exactly like the lampshade on the floor lamp next to my bed—narrow at the top and opening out—and, behind the goat, emerging from the shadows, the most beautiful woman he had ever seen, completely naked. Then the grotto began pulsing with a strange light. They stared at him, woman and goat. He knew if he crossed the stream his life would be changed. He'd never see his parents again, or maybe even the Greenies. The woman smiled invitingly but the goat hissed and out of its lampshade skull came poison smoke. My father turned and ran, onto the next wonder and adventure. Although I'm sure I asked about them, they never appeared in the stories again.

After that I couldn't look at the lamp without seeing the goat. It had two simultaneous beings. In the daylight, it was the lamp *and* the goat or the goat functioning as a lamp, and at night when the light was turned out it became the goat, perfectly still, an immobile outline permanently suspended in the instant before it would start to move and spume poison smoke. It sent a chill through me from toes to scalp, an awful thrill that was finally too much, and made me feel like I was spinning wildly in outer space. But when my father was sitting on the edge of the bed with his elbows on his knees, I could see his white shirt in the dark, I could feel the pressure of his hips, and that contact grounded me enough so that no matter how scared or crazy I became I wanted him to keep telling me the stories.

He didn't tell them often—each time had to be a special treat. And each time, before he would begin, he'd ask me if I believed in the Greenies. I had to say yes to get a story, to say I believed that this fabulous world was going on inside the earth even as he spoke. I didn't believe it, then I said I did, and as the word left my mouth I believed and didn't believe at the same time—like the goat-lamp. It was secret life. It was my father's secret life. He had made it from the basic stuff of the Old Testament, Buck Rogers, and H. Rider Haggard (*King Solomon's Mines*)—his favorite author—but also from his own childhood memories, probably some of the fondest he had, of being brave and adventurous, exploring caves by himself. Although he was the storyteller in our family, he almost never told me anything about *his* father, who was an alcoholic (like himself)—his father's absence from his stories only now seems significant to me. The stories were cautionary and instructional, exemplifying courage I was meant to emulate, invariably dramatizing his lonely battle with the world. He was always alone in them. Clearly, that was his memory of himself—or, more accurately, my memory of his memory of himself, communicated to me most powerfully in the Greenie stories (hybrids of memory and fantasy that they were): the hero against a hostile world. My dad was the hero. I absorbed the message like a soft little sponge, the way only a child can. I wanted to be like my dad. I wanted to be the hero, too.

But why tell this story of these stories? In a remarkable essay about his father in his almost-forgotten book of autobiographical essays, *Court of Memory*, James McConkey writes, "Memory, which gives us our identities, can, by an act of grace, release us from ourselves to an outpouring of its most hidden contents." My father's stories—his memory and identity—wounded me almost too deeply for words but also gave me life. They are engraved in me. Stories are the way we articulate ourselves to ourselves, as well as to one another. We tell hundreds of stories every day. Through their agency we make the amorphous, inexhaustible inner into the shapely, provisional outer. They are an irreplaceable way of knowing and mode of social intercourse (notwithstanding our dominant "efficient" scientific models of knowledge and social organization). Their material is the material of memory, which is generative, not a passive lump of stuff. One does not take a memory and make it into a story. Memory itself makes the story—and, as McConkey implies, we can be released not only *by* its story but also *to* it. Memory is both the subject and predicate of which we are the objects.

In this regard, the only difference between fiction and nonfiction is how faithful the writer must be to memory and how willing he is to rein it in when it gallops toward fantasy, for which it's also the source. Surely writing fiction—and reading it—can also produce that graceful release McConkey is talking about. Every reader of this essay has experienced the rapture of reading a piece of writing that *takes* you, an experience of art that probably reproduces an experience in life—of being "flooded" by memory, of tapping into an underground stream that seems simply to burst forth. But memory is always there, implicitly telling us what to feel and think, what we like and don't, who we are. "Memory . . . gives us our identities": we don't have memory: it has us—as if it were a container and an engine in which we are also contained, by which we are driven. How

·   ·   ·   ·   ·   ·   ·   ·   ·

deeply we are formed by what happens to us, whom we're born to, the previous generations who live in us. We are probably also what happened to them, even if we don't know what that is or even who they were, shards embedded in stories and chromosomes. No wonder we are such mysteries to ourselves. Our feelings are grounded in sources that will elude us no matter what reductive psychoanalytic explanations we construct to manage them or how many ingenious drugs are designed to alter them. "The eye sees what it has been given to see by concrete circumstances," wrote Flannery O'Connor, "and the imagination reproduces what, by some related gift, it is able to make live." How that moment of seeing the goat-lamp shaped me exceeds my powers of analysis, but, in O'Connor's terms, maybe not the power of imagination—by becoming part of a story.

The discipline of writing includes a special opportunity for the writer as a person to make an interpersonal object that not only expresses his feelings but also embodies them, that makes them both accessible to him and strangely independent of him. This is writing's gift to the writer and, like all large gifts, it carries a large obligation. O'Connor again: "In the act of writing, one sees that the way a thing is made controls and is inseparable from the whole meaning of it. The form of a story gives it meaning which any other form would change." It's precisely this that distinguishes rendering from remembering—or reporting, which is merely remembering with a pen in your hand (a tape recorder, in the case of the celebrity memoir). To use Henry James's favorite term for it, the writer has to "do" the thing he writes about. Through this "doing," the writer's unfathomable, private feelings are transformed into apprehensible, shared language. Such a complete transformation could happen in talk if talk weren't ephemeral, local, and unrevisable, if what was discovered in talk were worked over and made palpable (the way James worked over dinner-party-conversation "donnees" into novels). It's this lack of writing's discipline applied to subjects that require the utmost discipline that make bad memoirs so bad and afternoon talk shows so embarrassing—not, as some newspaper book critics have asserted, the subjects themselves. Shame becomes a circus act on Jenny Jones, but in the hands of a writer like Kafka (or O'Connor, or James, or Chekhov, or Shakespeare—the list could be extended to every great writer we have) it is an essential and inexhaustible subject, given a shape we can understand and deeply need to understand. It becomes social, public, part of shared culture, and thereby takes on significance. Whereas, left to fester and gnaw one isolated psyche, shame is only murderous. Did Kafka save his life by writing? Maybe not, but he has helped to save others. Mine, for one.

The most surprising personal aspect of writing my autobiography was discovering the emotional weight of events I had thought not so important to me. Because they were important to the story, they demonstrated how important they were to me. People I knew only briefly affected me more than I had ever guessed. It was as if the story itself called them up from the depths and showed me how to see them. Some of them I had almost forgotten, submerged in that underground stream of memory that the daily concentration of writing tapped into. My narrative—"the telling of events in time"—formed itself from the events memory had to tell.

But I also shaped the narrative, and, in this regard, I was continuously interacting with memory. By reading what I wrote, I perceived certain subjects—shame (and its compulsive sexual expression) prominent among them; growing up male, Catholic, and white in America; the hellish economic pressure on a middle-class family; a boy's love/ hate of his alcoholic father—and these subjects became the book's subject much more than what happened to me, which matters only as illustration, one instance of how these subjects impinged on one of many individual and unrepeatable lives: a testimony not a confession. The subjects became a principle of selection from the mass of all that happened to me, all the people I knew, all that was said or thought; and this principle, if I may call it that, pushed and pulled against incidents and characters that insisted on being part of the story. As Nabokov put it, "The following of thematic designs through one's life should be the true purpose of autobiography." This requires the exercise of the autobiographer's critical faculties, and the more talented a critic he is of his own life the better his book is likely to be—a talent he must exercise more explicitly than the novelist, and more certainly, since his misconceptions will be everywhere evident. In O'Connor words, "The writer has to judge himself with a stranger's eye and a stranger's severity. . . . No art is sunk in the self, but rather, in art the self becomes self-forgetful in order to meet the demands of the thing seen and the thing being made."

But is this really possible when the writer's own life is the subject? Can autobiography ever be "self-forgetful," as O'Connor rightly asserts art must be? It can only if the life of the story is the main thing—the life of the story, paradoxically, *not* the life of the autobiographer, which is merely the raw material of the story. The autobiographer must be mindful of the prerogatives and imperatives of the story in every way a novelist must be, and

. . . .

must be equally faithful to it, and finally no less able to enter the points of view of the characters at their specific times and places, especially his own. My task was not only to make the reader feel how it felt to be me; it was to make me feel how it felt to be me. In the act of writing, I relived the experience I was writing about—and I also didn't, because it was also becoming language, with the frustration and exhilaration which always accompanies that. When I lived those experiences as a child and teenager and young man there was plenty of frustration and precious little exhilaration, and none of it of the writerly kind. I felt lost and indeed was lost, never for a moment imagining that it all would someday become "material." Now the conditions of my life had changed. I was an adult (finally), no longer literally at the mercy of the conditions I was dramatizing. The writing helped me to be no longer at the mercy of these conditions emotionally, either—the release McConkey calls an act of grace. I needed the task of rendering my life, a contract with the reader which obliged me to honor the facts. I knew the gift of the story was wrapped in what actually happened (as memory remembered it and writing might render it)—the gift of the story to me and, I hoped, to the reader. "The reader" was oddly and exclusively *in* the act of writing itself. I wrote to the book, to the story, not to any person, real, imagined, or hypostatized. The aesthetic and ethical relationships between me and this reader-in-the-writing were identical: getting it down right was right.

Needless to say, however, this put me in conflict with myself—between me as a writer and as a person—over the revelations the story contained, that this story had to contain in order to be told. There was no avoiding that. As William Maxwell said in an interview,

> Sometimes I have suffered the torments of the damned in describing real people, where I was sure that I was, perhaps, causing pain. And in this struggle the artist won out. There was a point at which I would not give up something that I knew was right. Aesthetically. And artistically.

And he was talking about fiction, with its built-in ethical safety valve. No reader confuses Ishmael with Melville, or Nick Carraway with F. Scott Fitzgerald, or the unhappy husband who narrates "The Kreutzer Sonata" with Tolstoy (except the U.S. Post Office Department, which wouldn't deliver the American newspapers that serialized it, and State Senator Theodore Roosevelt who denounced its author as a "sexual moral pervert"). But the narrator of an autobiography, in the reader's mind, *is* the author—not just the writer, but also the person, in the flesh, who pays his taxes and shops for bagels.

This identification for the writer is both aesthetically and ethically perilous. "How could this guy publish this about his wife?" is not a question that occurs these days to most readers of "The Kreutzer Sonata." But such questions naturally do occur to readers of autobiographies, and they are much muddled at present in this atmosphere of promiscuous exposure à la Jenny Jones and the shame circus, the deadbolt linkage of information and promotion that pervades our media culture, in which what people are saying seems invariably connected to something they're selling (vide the Author Book Tour, apparently pioneered in our era by—who else?—Jacqueline Susann). Why should autobiographers be expected to be disinterested when nobody else seems to be? Much less about the representation of one's self and one's life, with its potential effects on one's well-being? Why should we not read autobiographies, especially ones that deal with intimate subjects and personal revelations, as mere "tell-alls," "domestic confessionals," and "autopathographies" (to cite just three hostile journalistic coinages): an inherently repugnant form of narcissistic merchandising, self-display, and self-promotion?

The book itself has to answer such questions—formally, in *its* character and tone—not the writer, on talk shows or anywhere else. If the writer's privacy is sacrificed for the book's intimacy, it may be worth it if the book is worth it, although that will not relieve "the torments of the damned" he may suffer, since how can he ever be sure his book is worth it? How can he compare his family's feelings to the good his book does and is? Books and people are not comparable. But the terms of art and life are deeply entangled, as they are in the writer himself as an artist and a human being. In my experience, there are no formulas to answer the ethical questions that arise when publishing an autobiography, except to ask for the permission of the people whose lives are exposed by it, much less the questions that arise while writing it, at moments when the ethical wages unconditional war on the aesthetic. The autobiographer's failure to win the reader's suspension of disbelief is perhaps even more deadly than the novelist's. He is condemned to tell his story in the first person, which complicates his problems no end. Just getting off center stage so the story can speak is a daunting technical and temperamental challenge that demands, among other things, preternatural psychological tact. Self-consciousness is as fatal as the lack of it, especially in the intricate business of self-portrayal. An excessively proprietary interest in his main character (himself) will sink his story like a pair of concrete boots. Any autobiographer who does not constantly torment himself with the question, "Is this interesting to anyone else?" is probably going to write a book that isn't. Without invention, he must fascinate us as much as a novelist with the endlessly interesting interactions between character (people) and plot (what happens to them), just as we are fascinated in and by our own lives.

How intimate should a story be? As intimate as it has to be, is the only answer I know. Each age has its idea of decorum, although we have come to expect art to violate it, so that the violation is sometimes now mistaken for the art and romanticized as "transgression." On the other side, the genteel tradition of criticism has always confused the beautiful and the agreeable, and the value of privacy with the conventions of secrecy. Maybe because most of my childhood reading was done in bed, alone in the halo of a small overhead lamp that seemed to define the circumference of the world, and I had heard my father's stories about the Greenies in a dim nightlight-lit bedroom, storytelling will forever be to me a most intimate act: the writer's voice is inside my head, inside me. The writer's consideration for me is shown not in sparing me his shame but in rendering his story clearly and palpably—"immediately, instantaneously graspable," in Chekhov's words—so that, most paradoxically in the case of autobiography, the writer seems to disappear into the details. "Released to an outpouring," "self-forgetful in order to meet the demands of the thing seen and the thing being made," he becomes his book, the story itself.

I haven't read Kathryn Harrison's *The Kiss* or Frank McCourt's *Angela's Ashes*, but I do know that Harrison's book is "about" incest and McCourt's is "about" his impoverished childhood in Limerick with his alcoholic mother (and includes her incestuous affair with her cousin). I know this despite not watching television or afternoon talk shows. This sort of sound-bite information seems to be in the air itself. Unfortunately, it's mistaken for knowledge—a natural mistake since we are forced to process so much information all the time. Humans, the learning animal, have adapted to this condition of daily life in most of the world. But it's a particularly unfortunate mistake when applied to books, although publishers encourage it and apparently believe they have to (and have to include marketing directors in their publishing decisions). Such information says less about a book than a Pepsi commercial says about Pepsi because a book is a more complicated mental and emotional experience than a soft drink, but the mechanism is the same, and this kind of thinking—this adaptation to info-glut—may now be the largest single obstacle between the writer and reader: It may be keeping some of the best books from being bought, published, and even written, and almost certainly affects how people read (or, more often, don't). To know Kathryn Harrison's book is about incest is to know almost nothing about it. Other books, especially fiction and poetry without identifiable and startling subjects, are less easily mistranslated into information and therefore do not enter the air at all.

This said, once a book is in a reader's hands, its relationship to him seems potentially the same as it ever was. It can teach not what to think and feel but how to think and feel. That some readers seek personal stories in reaction to a depersonalized culture in which institutional sources of authority are suspect may partially account for the so-called "memoir explosion." Autobiography is only more obviously "personal" than poetry or fiction, but it is finally always about memory, and as much about the moment of recollection as the moment being recalled—the presentness of the past and the pastness of the present, which every person must work out for himself over and over again if he wants a chance to be happy or useful or available to the ordinary pleasures of life. Other people's lives are interesting to us, but in this singular respect every good autobiography is also our own, a tale of the tribe that does for us what stories have always done.

Shame and Forgetting in the Information Age

. . . .

by

CHARLES BAXTER

> We have transformed information into a form of garbage.
> NEIL POSTMAN

1. IN MEMORY OF TOM, MY BROTHER

In April 1998, my brother Tom died, at the age of fifty-nine. He died in his sleep, of a heart attack, one day after his fifty-ninth birthday. He had been afflicted with bad health for some time, including congestive heart failure, renal failure, diabetes, cancer, and narcolepsy. He once fell asleep at the wheel and had to crawl out of his wrecked car and a drainage ditch to the nearest house. His financial affairs were a calamity. Faced with these problems, he was almost perversely upbeat. Every week over the phone I'd ask him how he was, and he'd say, "Not too bad for an old man!"

Tom was an outcast of the information age. Perhaps every family has one. He was ours. He had trouble in school (and he went to a lot of schools) because he could not learn printed information easily. Reading and writing often defeated him, and they did so before the culture had begun to employ the phrase "learning disability," and before this society had become dependent on computers. He had a computer and claimed he didn't know how to use it. For years, long after I had begged him to stop, he would introduce himself exuberantly as "the dumb brother." I was stricken by this phrase, made heart-sick by it, and by his efforts to turn this source of shame into an identifying badge.

Forgetting was shameful to him, and he felt it marked him for life.

His spelling was atrocious. He wrote in a scrawl. Much of my writing made very little sense to him, except for the stories that he recognized and in which he figured, and there were many. I wrote about him all the time. He was my muse for a while. He never forgot anyone he ever met, and he never forgot a story, witnessed or heard. He listened to stories and told them expressively, with awe and wonder. As long as he could function in the world, he was a salesman, a manufacturer's rep, a job in which he could put his storytelling capacities to use. He didn't—almost everyone said this about him—have a mean bone in his body.

His father—his and mine—died in 1948 when Tom was nine years old, and at the funeral some man, some friend of the family, told Tom, "You're *not* going to cry, are you." It wasn't a question; it was an order. "He told me to stuff it," Tom said later. And stuff it he did, with food.

Where do you go, what do you do, if you can't manage the printed information that we churn out? What becomes of you? What if you can't stand it? Melville's Bartleby starved in the Tombs. My brother took the opposite tack. He ate. He overate. He took it, the food, all in. He became large and unseemly; he became so big that when he came into the room, any room anywhere, people helplessly stared at this huge tottering man. He stuffed it and then he went on stuffing it. He absorbed it. He fought his shame (he always ate in secret, out of sight, preferably in the dark) by eventually calling attention to it: He began wearing pink sportshirts and kelly green trousers and rainbow suspenders. By his mid-to-late forties, he was unemployable, defeated by his exasperated difficulties with his appearance and with the printed word.

He was among the ranks of those who cannot easily process written information, the data-disabled. There's a large number of these people around, and no one likes to talk about them. They are a great scandal to our sensibilities. We have a myth that education will help them get on their feet. For some of them, yes. But for many, many others, education is the wall they can't get over, or through.

My brother had a storehouse of stories. If an experience had been witnessed and reported to him, he could remember the narrative in detail and tell it again. I'll repeat this for emphasis: he never forgot anyone. He loved to tell stories about how he had recognized someone who couldn't recognize him, who had forgotten who he was. It was his special triumph never to forget a name or a face, and he was amused by my own difficulty in remembering names. He thought it was a telling commentary on the sort of person I was, and am, that I had such difficulties. He was amused that I forgot human beings but remembered what I had read. However, if it—the information—arrived on paper, or on a screen, he'd lose track of the content. It wouldn't stick. With me, it did.

Nevertheless, he once could recite the words that Charley speaks over Willy Loman's grave, "a salesman don't put a bolt to a nut" speech, by heart. "All I have," my brother would say, "is a smile and a shoeshine." When I see him now, he is sitting at a table, telling an amazing story, a story that may or may not be true. He didn't always care if a story was literally true, but it had to be narratively useful and explain something that needed explaining.

By some miracle he never became embittered. He loved the world and loved God in a way that I refused to. He found the world quite wonderful, a fit place for stories. He was the first person to take me into a public library and to explain to me that each card represented a book. I didn't believe him. When I was eleven, I pestered him with questions about what happened on a date between the girl and the boy (I was completely mystified), and so, with his girlfriend's permission, he took me along the next time they went out, so he could show me how the thing was done. She let me hold her hand at the movie.

A few years ago he was officially put on the rolls of the disabled. He had been disabled almost from the start, and his various ambitions (to be ordained, to host a radio program) were frustrated by quizzes, tests, exams. All this terrible writing! It was inescapable. He even flunked out of radio school. Toward the end of his life—I can still hardly believe it—he became a freelance writer on the subjects of boating and outdoor recreation. It was a brave choice. It was like pitching your tent in the camp of the enemy. I don't know if he ever earned any money from it—I don't think he did— but it kept him busy.

He wanted to be remembered. To this end, he was horribly, shockingly, punitively generous to everyone. He was always giving something away. It was in his nature to do so, but it was also a request: please remember me; after all, I remember you. Every gift from him was a remembrance. He went bankrupt twice, mostly because he gave everything away.

When we went into his apartment after his death, the papers—all the documents and letters and magazines and bank statements and computer printouts and postcards and newspapers and ranks of unread how-to manuals and books and directories and reference books—were stacked and stashed everywhere. It rose, in great piles, almost to the ceiling. The air was bad. The papers had absorbed all the oxygen, and there was a rank smell of paper oxidizing, turning brown, like the smell of food cooking. He lived amid these documents. They surrounded him, like the foetid documentary accumulations in *Bleak House*. The apartment was stuffed with written material, all the paperwork of a lifetime, very little of it thrown out or recycled. It had befriended him. Because he couldn't hold it in his head, he kept it around and had learned to live with it. Besides, he couldn't bend over to pick it up.

We searched through it all. There was no will. He hadn't written one. As they say: all he had left behind were our memories of him. That, and the papers.

2. MEMORY, SHAME, AND FORGETTING: AN INTRODUCTION

Ann Arbor, Michigan, where I happen to live, is a small and rather tightly wound city where information processing is a major industry. Surrounded by farmland, the area is nevertheless dominated by the University of Michigan and by its intellectual, artistic, and athletic productions. A barn, not two miles from where I live, has M GO BLUE patterned on its roof shingles.

People here often take considerable pride in their minds and more particularly in their memories. The town is full of Know-It-Alls. It has to be. Standing in front of others, sporting their expensive ties and slightly askew accessories in classrooms or outside of them, my colleagues rattle off facts and figures and concepts and patterns while their students take notes. The virtuosi of knowledge, they are presumed to have—they *do* have—some authority because of what they know and what they remember. Their lives and their authority depend upon their ability to remember, and to remember their subjects in public. Having a private memory in a place like this one might be pleasant, but it is certainly beside the point, at least professionally. Private memories stay at home, or end up in a therapist's office.

The business of Ann Arbor (or Madison, or Berkeley, or Bloomington, any college or university town) is memory, cultural memory. Software, in every sense.

This may explain why I perked up, some months ago, as I was sitting in a local restaurant, when I heard two women in the next booth talking about memory. I bent over to eavesdrop, which is, in part, what I do for a living.

"How much memory have you got?" one of them asked the other.

"I don't know."

. . . .

"You don't *know*?" the first one asked. "You don't know how much memory you have? Didn't you ask the salesman?"

Of course they were not talking about their own minds. But it was an extraordinary conversation because its tone was so offhand, what one of my students once called "so *lunchtime*." In a way that even Marshall McLuhan might not have predicted, the mechanical extensions of humans have now apparently extended to our brains, and more particularly to our memories. "Your memory" can now in casual conversation refer to your computer's memory rather than your own.

This usage signals a conflation in the way that we think about the data we remember, as opposed to what we would call "our memories." "Our memories" are memories of our experiences in narrative form. They are probably not in the external computer unless we are keeping a journal or writing a memoir, in which case only the words are there. Data, by contrast, the proliferating facts and figures, can easily be stored.

Confusion about the two forms of memory is spreading and manifesting itself in peculiar ways, most peculiarly in what might seem to be its opposite, a huge desire or need to forget, a kind of fetishizing of amnesia. *Strategic amnesia* might be an appropriate phrase to describe how we are coping with information-glut, what David Shenk in a recent book on the subject called "data smog."

Strategic amnesia has everything to do with the desire to create or destroy personal histories. It has everything to do with the way we tell stories. As I write, it is smearing into unintelligibility the daily tableaux of public and political life. In this sense, narrative dysfunction and strategic amnesia are conniving, and have joined hands.

This is complicated and perplexing and needs to be approached slowly and with caution, not to say alarm.

We read and are told every day that our industrial economy has shifted in the last two decades toward the production of information. The manufacture of goods has been exported to a large degree and displaced by the mass production of data. The technology of data processing has increased exponentially year by year, resulting in high-speed forms of planned obsolescence in software programs (Windows, etc.) and in the computers themselves. The only frustrating limit to this technology, one CEO told me, is the speed of light, which is now too slow.

The easy mass access to the Internet has resulted in the rapid trading of

)rmation and the public postings of semiprivate and occasionally lurid
___terials in homepages and web sites. Furthermore, a large proportion of
the population works with, or is at least familiar with, information technology. We are all (well, most of us) computer users now. Many of us have
to spend the day in front of screens, moving the information around or
creating new information.

There is more information all the time. No one can absorb all the information. No one wants to. The day ends, not with physical exhaustion, but with data-fatigue or data-nausea. Information on a screen is
subtly different from information gleaned from books, although no one
has been completely clear about the nature of this difference. Because
there's always more information, an information explosion, but a limited capacity to absorb it or even to know what information is essential
and what information is trivial, anxiety often results, data-anxiety. What
do you need to know, what do you need to absorb, what do you need to
remember? Who can say? No one can keep up. No one is in a position to
tell you.

Given such a situation, every place where computers reign is like Ann
Arbor. You can process information perfectly well in a farmhouse in
North Dakota. In an information society, large sectors of the population,
to survive, have had to acquire some competency in handling data, organizing it, moving it around, displaying it, and disposing of it.

A proliferation of information causes information-inflation. That is,
every individual piece of information loses some value given the sheer
quantity of other information. Some information turns quickly into
garbage. Bad information may well force out good, in a Gresham's Law of
data processing.

The tremendous quantities of data—much of it trivial or even sub-
trivial—have created new forms of competency, having to do with both ar-
ranging the data and remembering it.

Remembering data and remembering an experience are two very different activities. It is possible that the quantity of data we are supposed to
remember has reduced our capacity to remember or even to have experiences; this turn of events was predicted by Walter Benjamin in the 1930s.
What meaning does forgetfulness possess in an information age?

IS IT FORGETFULNESS OR IS IT ALZHEIMER'S?
Advertisement headline in the *New York Times*
for a prescription drug, Cognex, to aid memory

. . . .

The signs of anxiety over forgetfulness have been turning up every-where lately, but most prominently, for me, in television commercials and newspaper ads. One recent such commercial, shown nationally, begins with documentary footage of a young woman in a large stadium singing the Canadian national anthem. After about ten seconds, she begins to fluff her lines. A pause, while she looks embarrassed and shamefaced. She then stops singing. Cut to a voice-over, an announcer saying, "Everybody needs a good night's sleep to perform well." On the screen, we see a shot of the product: a mattress. Memory-anxiety makes for good business.

Prescription drugs that aid the memory, so-called "cognitive en-hancers," are touted in full-page ads in the *New York Times*.

The phobia about forgetting has entered the run of daily conversation. A colleague in my department, forgetting my name as we meet in the hall-way, turns beet red from embarrassment and says that it must be the onset of Alzheimer's. Another friend, having forgotten her keys in her office, says that she is in fact worried not so much about the keys but about her memory slips. These slips are commonplace, she says, but they are causing her depressive spells. She can't stop talking about it. Clearly she is obsess-ing about her mental competence. Time and again, I have seen friends and colleagues lose their trains of thought in meetings and then blush and stammer and apologize, as if their professional standing had suddenly been endangered.

Many people seem to believe that remembering is simply a matter of willpower.

During an enormous stadium concert by the band R.E.M., Michael Stipe, the lead singer, apologizes to the audience, thousands of us, for having the lyric sheets to the songs he sings placed on a music stand in front of him.

In an information age, forgetfulness is a sign of debility and incompe-tence. It is taken as weakness, an emblem of losing one's grip. For anyone who works with quantities of data, a single note of forgetfulness can sound like a death knell. To remember is to triumph over loss and death; to forget is to form a partnership with oblivion. And in our time, the for-mer president, Ronald Reagan, has become the central figure, the genius loci, the brawny poster-child, of forgetfulness.

Reagan's most recognizable feature during his administration involved the conjunction of ahistoricism, rigid beliefs, self-indulgence, and in-tractable memory loss about details. When it suited him, and sometimes when it didn't, Reagan forgot. It was characteristic of Reagan to say, "I don't remember." Reagan's tendency to get history wrong, to render it imaginary, to discredit history altogether, slides imperceptibly into his double-dealing in the Iran-Contra affair, his forgetfulness and disavowals of responsibility, his social ethos of self-interest and selfishness, and, ultimately, into his final data-free twilight. In this sense, Reagan managed to contradict the principle that I laid out a few paragraphs ago: his forgetfulness, far from making him incompetent, *enabled* him to be the sort of president he was; it set him free from responsibility for his actions. For a while, he made forgetfulness *work*. Forgetfulness means that your mind may have crashed. It may, paradoxically, set you free.

Reaganism, understood as the proving ground of historical amnesia, strategically ignored the past in favor of a wasteful and an self-indulgent present. With Reaganism, forgetting aided and abetted power.

> Don't stop thinking about tomorrow.
> Don't stop—it'll soon be here . . .
> Yesterday's gone, yesterday's gone.
> *"Don't Stop" by Fleetwood Mac's Christine McVie played during the Democratic Convention nominating Bill Clinton*

With respect to the past, Clinton carries on the tradition started by Reagan. The disavowals of responsibility (Clinton denies; he never forgets) give to the Clintonian past the same aura as the Reagan past: it becomes unreadable and unintelligible. In a sort of postmodern political version of *Les Misérables*, Clinton turns into a presidential Jean Valjean pursued by the relentless Inspector Javert, Kenneth Starr. But this time around, there is something fishy about Clinton's pose of innocence and Starr's pose of righteousness. Starr, whatever his political associations might be, is in the position of trying to reconstruct and narrativize Clinton's past not for the purposes of truth but to serve political ends, and Clinton, like Reagan before him, seems to be eager to make that past go away. The Starr Report, not surprisingly, makes the case against Clinton by constructing what it calls "The Narrative."

Clinton is a representative figure of our time because he remembers huge quantities of data but also seems eager to slip large sections of the past into the trash icon, so that he can indulge himself. Clinton seems to be able to bury the past without demonstrating visible shame. (Nixon, at least, dependably broke out into a sweat whenever the cameras were trained on him.) After each new revelation, Clinton goes back on TV, smiling, looking the same as ever. "Yesterday's gone" is a phrase from political progressivism and, in this case, from the recent and excitingly narcotic political rhetoric of debauchery and deniability, just like the now-classic "mistakes were made." His high approval ratings suggest that nobody really minds, that, in fact, the American people secretly approve. Clinton has become a hero of selective data management.

3. ON INFORMATION AND MEMORY: WALTER BENJAMIN

In his essay "The Storyteller" (1936), collected in *Illuminations*, Walter Benjamin makes a series of points about the relation between information and experience. In a calm tone that belies his apocalyptic intent, Benjamin argues that the explosion of information in the Modern Age is denying us something precious: "the ability to exchange experiences." That is, storytelling.

"Experience," Benjamin says, "has fallen in value." To paraphrase his argument: you don't want to hear about my experiences anymore. Nor am I usually in a mood to tell you about them. Why? First of all, because much of my experience feels blank, terrible, or unchanging. Benjamin here uses the example of mute shell-shocked soldiers coming back from World War I. Secondly, I'm not having experiences in my day-to-day life: instead, I'm absorbing or processing information. "Information," Benjamin says, "proves incompatible with the spirit of storytelling. If the art of storytelling has become rare, the dissemination of information has had a decisive share in this state of affairs."

Benjamin goes on, in a wonderfully suggestive but somewhat unclear manner, to differentiate between a memory for information and a memory for experiences. His implication is that the coming information-glut will force experience—and storytelling generally—into a corner and additionally force it to resort to extremes.

Imagine a person who spends all day in a windowless office or cubicle, copying or moving information. Let us whimsically call this person Ms. Bartleby. Ms. Bartleby must go to sales conferences and talk about all the new ideas and theories and projections, and she must be absolutely current in the resources and techniques of data management and document preparation and presentation, and she must remember much of what has been said to her over her cell phone and what has appeared on her computer screen, and she must check her pager every half hour. Whatever the job is that she must do, they want it done yesterday.

Nevertheless, Ms. Bartleby comes home, at the end of the day, feeling blank. The only experiences she has had, during the whole week, are those that seem to be empty of actual experiential content (unless you count that turbulence that her flight encountered over—what was it?—Cleveland?). The data leaves no experience-memory in her head. She comes to the end of the week craving a drink or a drug. At least that's an experience. Maybe she wants to do an extreme sport for a few hours on Saturday. She may have spiritual yearnings but no particular outlet for them. But she doesn't really want to talk about her work because she can't converse about it. She can only make statements about it. There aren't any stories there, unless her coworkers are seducing or cheating or harassing each other, always a possibility.

Benjamin's point about this is that our experiences have been reduced in number at the same time that the available mental space for them has shrunk. In an information age, our representative figure, Ms. Bartleby, is rich in information and poor in experience. She sits all day in front of screens at work, and then she sits in front of screens at home. If she has a baby, there's half a chance that the father will not aid the birth, but video-tape it. Instead of trusting his own memory, he'll record the event by means of mechanical reproduction, turning it into a spectacle on TV. Returning to Ms. Bartleby: she is going to put a huge amount of psychic pressure on the quality of whatever relationships she has, and there may be quite a few, as a result. She will feel terrible shame if she forgets any of the data she is supposed to master. And yet, if her life feels inadequate and shallow to her, that very forgetting, that very shame, may, through a quasi-Freudian reversal, also seem immensely attractive.

Forgetting and shame might just serve, under the immediate surface of consciousness, as an escape route of sorts.

Not "I prefer not to," but "I don't remember." Or, "I prefer not to" in the form of "I don't remember." Not remembering locates itself as an act of sabotage against mere data, of rebellion at the local level. It is memory's version of the Freudian slip.

Bartleby would only feel shame at not remembering if she felt that her job was really worth doing. If the job wasn't especially worth doing, if it was a Dilbert job, or if she had messed up and wanted to cover her tracks, forgetfulness would take on a positively Elysian aspect. It would put her right back into childhood. And there would be the example of Reagan. Reagan's forgetfulness gave him a certain innocence, a head-shaking self-deprecatory boyishness.

Clinton's boyishness has been remarked upon by everyone, and quite acidly by Bob Dole, who never looked much like a boy even when he was one.

4. SHAME, INNOCENCE, AND THE MEMOIR

The recent proliferation of memoirs has been viewed with alarm by literary and cultural pundits, who have claimed that all these memoirs are yet another manifestation of the ubiquitous viral narcissism at work in the American cultural body, identified by Christopher Lasch and several others. Well, maybe. But if we follow the lines sketched out decades ago by Benjamin, we might discover that the literary memoir is, like therapy, a local antidote to information-poisoning. It's a perfectly reasonable response to the devaluation and even destruction of personal experience. The memoir (along with journal writing) is one of the few places where experience-memory goes to take shelter and to be increased in value. The memoir is memory's revenge upon info-glut. Television cannot do it; movies cannot do it. If anything, they stand against the intimacy of personal experience in favor of spectacle.

Every memoir argues that a personal memory is precious. No other artistic form makes that argument with the same specificity or urgency.

After all, if you have a personal memory, what can you do with it? You can carry it around, or you can try to dispose of it. But the chances are that your memories will feel precious to you, and you may want to share them by narrating them. They constitute the story of your life, the key to your own narrative. Traumatic memories may be the exceptions. I will have more to say about this later.

Because of their value, personal memories are rarely treated with irony by the person who has them, at least in America. Irony, by metaphorically negating what has actually happened, would render your own memories and your life inchoate. Irony would be an auto-inflicted calamity when applied to one's own memories: it would be like putting oneself into liquidation. Memoirs tend to be earnest, even when they are lyric and comic. They exhibit loyalty to one's own past. Even Nabokov was dead serious about his past in *Speak, Memory*, no matter how much he applied the filigree. No one treasured a personal past more than he did.

What you remember is the key to who you are. This commonplace formulation excludes dismissive irony and the mere piling-up of information as techniques for memoir writing. Personal information must be

[margin note: personal must be converted into experience see p. 150]

converted into experience if it is to communicate anything, methodically disproving the bleakest of Benjamin's prophecies. If any writer can tell the story of his or her life, s/he has a chance of escaping from the suffering of a dysfunctional personal narrative. S/he is seeking to understand that suffering and to turn it into something readable and coherent and functional in a time of data-glut. As a result, *a memoir cannot be summarized.* It only works if it includes the details. There's no intimacy otherwise, and any memoir requires intimacy to convey its experiences.

[margin note: Huyssen]

American memoirs of the past two decades are some of the most powerful literary documents that we have created during this period, in part, I think, because they have taken seriously the condition of innocence and the subsequent corruption or fall from that innocence, and seen it in relation to storytelling. The memoir has saved a place for childhood and adult experience when everyone else in the professional-managerial class was trying to get rid of it. Memoirs are deeply involved with rites of initiation and with education. This is classic memoir territory, familiar from Augustine and Rousseau. To quote Robert Hass, "All the new thinking is about loss./In this it resembles all the old thinking."

[margin note: Robert Hass]

And yet these inquiries into innocence and its loss often appear to have another common theme. It is natural that a writer would want to write about parents, but recent memoirs seem to have reserved a special place for missing or empty or vacated or just bad fathers. Something has gone wrong with the fathers; there is something either shameful or absent about them.

Gertrude Stein, a sort of one-woman early-warning system, was one of the first to notice this phenomenon. In *Everybody's Autobiography,* published in 1937, she writes that, following the death of God, we are about to go into the era of the Bad Father. She names Hitler and Stalin as examples. "There is too much fathering going on just now and there is no doubt about it fathers are depressing."

Stein's own *The Making of Americans* is father haunted. So is Paul Auster's *The Invention of Solitude,* Mary Karr's *The Liars' Club,* Kathryn Harrison's *The Kiss,* Michael Ryan's *Secret Life,* Geoffrey Wolff's *The Duke of Deception,* Tobias Wolff's *This Boy's Life,* and Mary Gordon's *The Shadow Man: A Daughter's Search for Her Father.* Perhaps this is all historical coincidence. But I think not; I think something else is going on.

The fathers or stepfathers in most of these books are elusive. They distort their own histories, or empty them out, or tell tall tales, in order to create dysfunctional narratives, thereby increasing their own power and confusing their children. They take on the role of the storyteller in order to create puzzles and mazes rather than histories. To recapitulate my argument from a previous essay on the subject, narrative dysfunction (the phrase is C. K. Williams's) is the process by which we lose track of the story of ourselves, the story that tells us who we are supposed to be and how we are supposed to act. In a dysfunctional narrative, true accountability vanishes. No one seems to be responsible for anything, or else the wrong people are accused of what may not, in fact, have happened at all. This is usually a complex response to shame: incest (*The Kiss*), alcoholism (*Secret Life*), repressed family histories (*The Invention of Solitude*), or ethnic identity (*The Shadow Man, The Duke of Deception*). Shame comes first, but strategic forgetting follows closely behind.

In most of these books, the author is at pains to investigate history in order to understand it, to tell the truth after a father has lied about it or simply said nothing or pretended to forget it. What the fathers in these books have done is to gain the upper hand by telling an odd story or by staying silent. They remain figures of sometimes diabolical authority as long as the stories they tell falsify history or drain it of content.

Evading their own lives, they manage by means of dysfunctional narratives to disable the lives of their children, their listeners. Strategic amnesia replaces paternal accountability.

We are back to Reagan. These fathers institute a form of Reaganism at the local, domestic level.

If your memory of your experiences is precious, *then your father has, at least in a patriarchal culture, a special and almost sacred power to confirm a history.* He can also distort or corrupt history and the past and your place in it. The rise of the memoir, then, is not so much a sign of literary narcissism as it is an antidote to the widespread practice of dysfunctional narration within the family. Every memoir seeks to make a narrative functional again, to tell the truth about experience.

5. "MAYBE ERASURE IS NECESSARY": THE LITERATURE OF FORGETTING

The literature of the first three-quarters of this century is distinguished thematically by its efforts to go in search of lost time. A large number of the great texts of this century are, typically, heroic efforts at historical remembrance, reconstruction, recollection. Against our zest for destruction, they preserve the personal memory and the cultural artifact. They

. . . .

reconstruct. They hold on. They are our epics of conservation in the face of certain loss.

You would think that forgetting, the erasure of the specific, would be antiliterary and antihistorical—a counternarrative practice. You would think that there could be no such thing as a literature of forgetting, no such thing as a great epic of amnesia. The pages, by necessity, would all be blank. *Tout oublier, c'est tout . . . quelque chose.*

Everything would dissolve into a haze. It might begin as trauma or comedy but it would certainly end as nightmare.

Nevertheless, it's just possible that in the last part of the twentieth century, we are pioneering a new kind of literature, a literature of amnesia, as we assemble the fragmentary texts of forgetting. This new literature is probably one side effect of data-nausea, of which narrative minimalism may be another. If memory stands against death, forgetting stands against data. It's also one solution to the problem of trauma.

The first novel I remember reading that used forgetting as a consistent narrative device was Edmund White's *Forgetting Elena* (1973), much admired by Nabokov. After two hundred pages of comic antinarrative, the narrator, following the beautiful and mysterious Elena's death, remembers himself and his apparent storytelling task. Does he want to deliver the eulogy for Elena? His answer is, "I remember nothing. Who is Elena?" The end. It's as if Nick Carraway, after struggling unsuccessfully for two hundred pages to remember who Gatsby *was*, conclusively asked, in a moment of brilliant slack-jawed obtuse blankness, "Who is Gatsby?" The question isn't rhetorical; the character, by being forgotten, is gone, and the book, thank God, is over. It's a sort of camp triumph over Proustian monumentalism.

We stand here in the shadow of Beckett, the plays and novels made out of loss and emptiness and absence, of stories and texts for nothing, of *Imagination Dead Imagine*, of Beckett's claim that James Joyce had used the resources of memory and history, and that he, Beckett, would take the opposite course, the way of forgetting. We stand in the shadow of Maeterlinck's Mélisande in *Pelléas and Mélisande*, perpetually vague and beautiful, without any discernible history, demanding attention and love from everybody, unconversant, resigned, quiet, a catalyst for violence, erotic, and mutely hysterical .

In one form or another, writers of talent have devised a fictional poetics of forgetting, of momentary stories without a past: Douglas Cooper in *Amnesia*, Steve Erickson in *Amnesiascope*, Lydia Davis in *Almost No*

· · · · · · · · · ·

Memory, to name only a few examples. Dennis Cooper's narrator, at the end of *Guide*, says, untellingly, in his last sentence, following 176 pages of narrative, "You can basically forget about us." Meaning: you *should* forget about us. If you can. Just try.

The shame of forgetting. The necessity of it. What help is the data if you don't—if you can't and won't—remember the story? My last example is drawn from Tim O'Brien's 1994 novel *In the Lake of the Woods*. O'Brien's novel doesn't answer these questions, but it poses them ingeniously. The book's narrative is absolutely and conclusively dysfunctional: there's a way into it but no way out. Its characters disappear and ultimately vanish, and the book's project is to make their disappearances unanswerable and invisible. There may be an art, even a high art, to evasion; if so, this book practices it. The book is constructed to be unintelligible at its most crucial points, and I don't mean that as criticism.

In all truth, *In the Lake of the Woods* is a strange novel. It gives off an odor of sulphur. Its protagonist, John Wade, also known as "Sorcerer," has been in Vietnam and has been involved with the butchery at Thuan Yen, a place commonly known as My Lai. After his return to the United States, he runs for political office but is defeated when his past catches up with him. Following his defeat at the polls, he takes his wife Kathy up to Minnesota's Lake of the Woods. There, something happens to Kathy. She disappears. She may (or may not) have been killed by her husband, who may (or may not) have poured boiling water out of a teakettle all over her. He can't remember. In any case, John dutifully and despairingly searches for her once she's gone. At the end of the novel, he, too, disappears, hunting for her (the book, one might say, is *about* hunting), across the vast expanse of that lake. He vanishes over the horizon line of the narrative, and the prose ends, or maybe just stops, with a blizzard of questions.

Those are the bones of the story, and I have recounted them in a somewhat glib and offhanded manner, because they don't really account for much in the book. There is no final accounting here. It is as if every element in the tale had become hypothetical. The author is constantly disclaiming his own authority, yanking back events and episodes that were posited as actual. The protagonist and the narrative reel from one event to the next, blank-faced, almost criminally obsessive, traumatized.

In this novel, trauma everywhere infects the narrative order. The only certainty is that John Wade went to Vietnam and saw something there. Beyond that, epistemological frenzy, narrated in a somewhat deadpan manner, is the rule rather than the exception. Does John really love Kathy? The novel claims that he does, but the examples of this love are persistently hollow and overmiked, like someone shouting into a public-address system. Did he kill her? The implied narrator, at one point, finds this possibility *distasteful*. What are John's experiences? Whatever they are, they are so terrible—and the novel is quite clear about this particular fracturing—that they cannot be held in the memory. We arrive, by a tortuous and circuitous route, back at shame, as catalyst and curse.

As if to compensate for all this narrative vacancy, these holes in the story, the novel applies an interesting strategy, designed to fail. Using the narrator as a sort of classic investigator on the scene of the crime, the book at first subtly and then quite openly begins to subdivide, like a paramecium. One part of the book remains a traditional if evasive narrative of John and Kathy's experiences. The second part contains testimony and facts. To the trauma of the story, the book supplies evidence, testimony, witnesses, and tragicomic footnotes. The footnotes, of course, give the appearance of explaining something by providing pivotal evidence and data. "Pivotal evidence," however, is woefully insufficient. So is the data. Because the entire novel is in the form of an unsolved mystery, the footnotes constitute a wild-goose chase. There are intensely interesting discoveries along the way, but the whole journey eventuates in a mystifying absence.

The book, halfway through, begins to experience its own data-smog, a self-generated info-glut. Very cannily, it places this data-smog next to a traumatized and piecemeal history, which is both John Wade's and, by extension, America's. It's as if our recent annals are shot through, not with momentous events occurring in a stately historical manner, but with trauma: assassinations, massacres, unthinkable horrors enacted on a daily basis. Yet another child enters yet another school and methodically kills his classmates, and the townspeople, on camera, say that it's senseless. Someone else goes crazy somewhere and starts the killing spree. For these horrors there's no explanation and finally no adequate narration. In a fundamental way, there's no story. Fact are no help. Facts make it worse. They increase the pain by adding to the store of memory a set of claims that cannot fill up the hole left by traumatized subtraction. As O'Brien's narrator says, "Maybe erasure is necessary."

Tim O'Brien's novel is finally an example of what the critic Jerry Herron has described as "the humiliation of history." History is narratable as long as its events occur in some logical way, but when trauma and shame are introduced into the mix, history is corrupted from the inside. The one story my brother Tom could not tell was the continuing story of why he ate in the way he did. Against a shame that you cannot bear, your mind detaches itself from its own memory and sails off in the direction of a psychic Lake-of-the-Woods. It is the strategic amnesia of everyday life, both involuntary and willful.

All the computers in the world cannot remedy it.

NOTES

Walter Benjamin, "The Storyteller," in *Illuminations*. Edited by Hannah Arendt, translated by Harry Zohn (New York: Schocken Books, 1969): 83–110.

Jerry Herron, *AfterCulture: Detroit and the Humiliation of History* (Detroit: Wayne State University Press, 1993).

Neil Postman, quoted in David Shenk, *Data Smog* (San Francisco, HarperEdge, 1997).

American Nomad

. . . .

by

STEVE ERICKSON

There is a sort of blow to one's soul, Scott Fitzgerald once wrote, "that comes from within—that you don't feel until it's too late to do anything about it, until you realize with finality that in some regard you will never be as good a man again." A few sentences later he wrote the line about how, during a dark night of the soul, it is always three o'clock in the morning; and one night a few years ago, outside Coeur d'Alene in Idaho when it really *was* three in the morning, I began to understand that just as it is required of Americans to dream ridiculously, it is subsequently required that they succeed or fail ridiculously too, the success almost too grandiose or the failure almost too catastrophic to take seriously. Writing *The Crack-Up* at the age of thirty-nine, Fitzgerald had already begun his suicide of a sort, though perhaps that's unfair given the grace and heroism with which he struggled against it. Nonetheless, by then the distant beckoning green light at the end of *Gatsby* had pulled far out of Fitzgerald's view, along with the harbor where his dreams were docked; he was just beginning to see American failure for the nightmare it was, having already seen its success for the paradise it promised a young man, before that paradise was lost. Fitzgerald's crack-up was in L.A. It was probably just as well he wasn't staying in a motel outside Coeur d'Alene. L.A. either bought him a few years, if you want to look at it that way, or robbed him of another forty, if you want to look at it that way. At any rate it was a pretty good place to find out that there is no place worse than America to be prematurely on the downward slide of whatever your particular trajectory is.

That last time I was on the road, in the early Nineties, I went a little bit

.   .   .   .

insane. Once I was a traveler by nature, rootless by nature; but the last time I descended rootlessly into America I lost myself somewhere east of Montana, for reasons not worth going into now. If you want to know how crazy I was, I was this crazy: after cracking up, I fled as quickly as possible *to Las Vegas.* Anytime you go to Vegas to get *less* crazy, well, that's crazy. The psychosis of the American landscape accommodated just a little too easily the way in which all my dreams had come to seem lost or trivial, and the way that I had systematically cut myself off from everything and everyone so as to punish myself for having failed the life I had aspired to for so long.

Now back on the road some years later, in the fall of 1996, having driven 3,000 miles over the course of several weeks, I kept telling myself I wouldn't go crazy this time because, after all, this time I had a purpose to my journey. Though every time anyone asked me what it was—"Yes, but: if you're not actually writing about the presidential election, then what *are* you writing about?"—I babbled like an idiot. And I could feel the craziness lurking just down the highway, and I kept swerving to avoid it, taking obscure detours, hiding out in motels until I convinced myself the danger had passed. For most of the trip I had been playing a tape of Frank Sinatra memory-songs—"Last Night When We Were Young," "Everything Happens to Me," "When the Wind Was Green," "I See It Now"—but I wasn't playing those anymore, I had moved onto somewhat harder stuff, a lot of Dylan for a while, then a new live record of Kurt Cobain singing from beyond the white blast of the shotgun with which he took his life, and a new Patti Smith record, an American Songbook of the Dead, elegizing every mortal thing around us that has passed away, including Kurt Cobain. Somewhere just south of the Great Lakes there was a left turn on the map for Cahokia, the last great American city before the Old World found the New and presumed to call it new, now buried in the plains of southern Illinois.

In a perverse way I was covering the presidential campaign perfectly, since it had slipped the moorings of logic as easily as I had. A year before, I had been hired by *Rolling Stone* to write about the election like a novelist, a concept that went by the wayside somewhere between the doorway of Jann Wenner's office and his desk, before I ever stepped foot on the campaign trail; the assignment barely began before I was relieved of duty. But then I had this idea, not necessarily an inspiration but a perverse impulse that became more and more irresistible, that I would just go right on covering the campaign anyway. I would get in my car with my bogus press

badge and my bogus business cards and I would start driving, a bogus cor-
respondent without portfolio, and I would write the story of the campaign
the way I had wanted to in the beginning, and the way I had foolishly supposed in the beginning I was being hired to do, but now armed with
moonshine credentials and a surreptitious itinerary of my own making.
And I would keep on driving out deeper into America and into the last
years of the Twentieth Century, on one last rampage through the national
asylum just to make one last observation, one last comment, or even to tell
just one last lie, just as long as no one expected from me one last answer.

At the outset of the fall campaign my strategy had seemed clear-cut,
which was to plant myself in the bull's-eyes of Michigan and Ohio and
wait for the campaign to come to me. "Well," John Buckley, Bob Dole's
communications director, had told me in late August, "if you're in Michigan and Ohio, you'll be seeing a lot of us." In yet one more example of my
own naiveté, in terms of following the campaign I had hoped Buckley was
my ace in the hole; I had met him briefly seven years before at an *Esquire*
party in New York. At the time he had just written a generous review of
one of my novels for the *Wall Street Journal*. The slightly eccentric and
iconoclastic nephew of William Buckley, he was a novelist himself and
former rock critic; around that time he was quoted as saying, "I don't see
any contradiction between being a conservative interested in economic
growth and a strong national defense, and going to see the Pixies on a
given weekend night," and my reaction at the time had been twofold.
First, that he was absolutely right, that it was small-minded and bigoted to
assume such a contradiction; and second, that of course it was a complete
contradiction, given the Right's clear, documentable predisposition to
judge experience rather than understand it. I don't think even Buckley
would argue that the Pixies, whose most memorable song was called "De-
baser," were what Bob Dole or Bill Bennett or Pat Buchanan or Ralph
Reed had in mind when making the case for a more wholesome popular
culture.

Nonetheless, seven years later Buckley seemed open to my entreaties
concerning the campaign. By the middle of September, having reached
Grand Rapids, I was calling his office on a regular basis; I didn't take it personally when, sooner instead of later, he started not calling back. By now
campaign reporters were openly complaining in print and on the air about
phone calls routinely unreturned by the Dole campaign and an unprecedented level of restriction the campaign had imposed upon the press. Not
really in the business of reporting anymore, I could afford to be under-

. . . .

standing about it: the Dole candidacy was either collapsing altogether or coming apart at all the hinges and joints, whichever metaphors of gravity or entropy or centrifugal force you wanted to apply to the situation. The problem with my plan of focusing on Michigan and Ohio was that Dole was focusing on them with something less than the single-mindedness I had expected; all you had to know about how this campaign was going was that while Clinton was holding wildly enthusiastic outdoor rallies on Lake Shore Drive in Chicago, Dole was frantically touring prisons in Arizona, the most congenitally Republican state in the union except for Utah, trying to reinforce his credentials there as a good law-and-order Republican. In breezy response the President not only picked up the endorsement of the largest police union in the country—the first time ever for a Democratic nominee—but had the chutzpah to visit Arizona himself, personally dropping in to pay his respects to Barry Goldwater, who was in the hospital recovering from a small stroke and was quoted in a major newsweekly as saying that while he supported Dole, he had to allow as how, all in all, Clinton had really been a pretty good president. Conservative Republicans whose first political hero had been Goldwater now fumed privately that he had gone senile. Perhaps so, but it was a plague of senility that had descended on not only Goldwater, not only the police, not only the country's leading CEOs, who as a group also endorsed Clinton as "good for business and good for America," but Arizona as a whole, which in fact would vote for a Democrat on Election Day for the first time since Harry Truman.

So it was not so easy catching up with the Dole campaign in Michigan and Ohio, because the campaign was just as often in Arizona and New Hampshire and South Carolina and Alabama and Texas *and Kansas*, a slew of Republican strongholds neither strong nor necessarily holding for the Republican nominee. Along with Arizona, New Hampshire would ultimately go for Clinton. Though in the end Dole would do better than his shambles of a campaign had the right to expect, losing by only half the margin predicted in the polls—decisive to be sure, but not abject humiliation—and taking nineteen states, virtually all of them in the South and the midwestern plains that I had crossed between California and Illinois, in late October Dole had only seven states he could comfortably consider in his pocket. These were led by Mississippi, the thirty-first largest in the union, followed by such teeming powerhouses as Utah (thirty-fourth), Nebraska (thirty-seventh), Idaho (forty-second), Alaska (forty-eighth), Wyoming (fiftieth), and, yes, probably Kansas (thirty-second), all with thirty electoral votes between them. The only large states where he appeared to have any realistic chance were Texas and Florida, and it was only the most spectacular measure of how hopeless Dole's cause was that either was in question at all. In fact he would lose Florida.

"My wife Elizabeth and I have traveled to the scenes of many natural disasters over the years," Dole joked with crowds in early September. "That doesn't include my campaign, of course." By late October it didn't seem so funny. Organizationally the campaign certainly had the appearance of complete disarray, if the sudden upheavals of the schedule could be taken into account: the night Peter Jennings was announcing on his ABC evening newscast that Dole would be in Grand Rapids the next day, campaign headquarters in Washington was announcing that it was Jack Kemp who was going to be in Grand Rapids; Bob Dole would be in Lansing. Actually the next day it was Jack Kemp who was in Lansing and Bob Dole was in Detroit; and by the time one shifted gears in time to reach Detroit, Bob Dole was in Ohio. Then as America shuddered into the prematurely frigid autumn, and I hurtled ever more quixotically down the shores of Lake Michigan past the huge mansions of Nineteenth-Century lumber barons, and beaches of long-sunk shipwrecks and the bare branches of autumnal trees filled with huge glistening spider webs, the Dole campaign made the truly desperate and audacious decision to relocate itself for the duration to California, where no sane person could really believe the Kansan had a chance, one or two modestly—and fleetingly—encouraging state polls notwithstanding.

By now Dole's speeches about the economy and tax cuts gave way to harangues about drugs and even the old George Bush favorite, constitutional amendments to ban burning the flag. (Republicans never propose amendments to ban burning the Bill of Rights.) On only a barely subterranean level these speeches were really about the Sixties, for which Clinton offered such gossamer representation, what with Dole commercials showing the President on MTV some years earlier at his shit-eating worst, grinning that if he had the chance again he would take a good puff of the old devil weed just to let the kids know he was cool, and then the usual ridiculous retraction a few nights later to Barbara Walters. With a frenzy that belied the aura of calm decency he was trying to sell the country, Dole was trying to take America back to where it had all really gone wrong, thirty years before: he was Dole the Rememberer, keeper of the past's Better Days. Amazingly, before he switched back to talking about the tax cut, almost no one in the Republican camp seemed to notice that the drug issue

· · · · · · · · ·

showed signs of working for Dole, with the President's lead shrinking to below ten for the first time since the San Diego convention. There was a part of the collective American spirit that believed Dole was right, that something about the country *was* better back when all of us could feign a child's innocence together, beyond the reach of consequential choices, even if the country never seemed to believe that Dole was the one who could make it so again, or indeed that anyone could make it so again. The green light in Gatsby's harbor had disappeared altogether from view and, for better or worse, it was Bill Clinton, not Bob Dole, who was going to sail us to whatever port could still be reached.

That Bob Dole might be right, that Clinton might be, as the Republican nominee put it following the second presidential debate, a man who just talked in his slippery silver-tongued fashion of "promises he hasn't kept, votes he hasn't earned, goals he hasn't accomplished and virtues he hasn't displayed," was irrelevant. The American public was being notably hard-headed about the whole thing: not a single bumper sticker, in 2,500 miles from Los Angeles to Grand Rapids, for Clinton or Dole or Perot or Nader or Jesus or Elvis; not until I got into downtown Chicago did I finally see one for the President. And it might well have been that America was as content as the commentators suggested—"Look," my wife said on the phone, "maybe people just feel that things are *being taken care of*"—and certainly part of me wanted to believe it, and perhaps the part that couldn't believe it said more about me than it did about America. Perhaps part of being an American was refusing to accept that the country could ever weary of democracy, refusing to accept that a profound ennui could ever settle into the American soul, that the wild fluctuations in less than half a decade from Bush to Clinton to Gingrich to Dole back to Clinton could ever be signs of a deep national madness rather than the constant and reasonable correction of a chosen course, refusing to accept that some romantic nonsense about green lights in the harbor didn't mean anything to people with children to raise and bills to pay and jobs to keep or lose, people who had their hands rather too full of real life to worry about an America of the abstract. For them the meaning of America was something to be lived, and lived day to day often with great difficulty, not airily contemplated or while aimlessly cruising the interstates.

Thus it could be argued that, to their credit, this was what both Clinton and Dole spoke to: not America the Ideal but America the Real. It might indeed be that the President of the United States was as empty as an echo chamber, expedient down to his soul; but it might also be that he was the perfectly responsive public servant democracy was invented to produce, and that it was typical of ideologues to contend that anyone who was not ideological was thereby devoid of all conviction, even as it was also clear that most ideologues became idealogues in the first place by putting the truth in the service of their biases rather than the other way around. Only to the Clinton-haters was it remotely contestable that, whatever other venal things might be true of him, Clinton did in fact seem to evince a true concern about people and share their pain, as it was always put so snidely by the cynics; and that, beyond that, he believed in whatever worked politically because what did not work politically accomplished nothing, and he believed in his own power and survival because without power nothing could be accomplished in any case.

As for Bob Dole, the final weeks of the campaign were nothing if not sad. If he did not necessarily deserve to be president, he certainly did not deserve these final weeks: the Republican Party he had served loyally to the point of near self-sacrifice in his 1974 reelection to the Senate, only three months after the resignation of his hero Nixon, whom he had continued to passionately defend when everyone else stopped, was now cruelly cutting him loose in an ultimately successful bid to hold Congress. Rather like Robert Lee after Pickett's Charge, watching his troops cut down and muttering, "It's my fault, all my fault," as the wounded and bleeding staggered back to camp, Robert Dole assumed responsibility accordingly, no matter that it wasn't Dole who might be losing the Gingrich Congress but that in fact it was the Gingrich Congress that had lost the Dole presidency. And for its part, the national press, now starved for carnage after years of piously bemoaning negative elections, splendidly outdid itself in its hypocrisy, sneering at a campaign so bland and polite, wondering aloud when Dole was going to "take the gloves off" and give the people the show they wanted, though in fact the people wanted nothing of the sort. The spectacle of a media that had written Bill Clinton off for dead after the debacle of November 1994—suggesting, as one had at the time, that Clinton should just spend the next two years of his presidency flying around in *Air Force One* and "enjoying life," like a man with a terminal illness who had a few moments left to smell the roses and put his affairs in order—now writing off Bob Dole, was a little outrageous even to those who stopped being flabbergasted by the press's arrogance long ago. Dole clung to his dignity as long as he could. When he finally took the bait in the second debate he did it rather awkwardly, reducing the attack on the President's character to the usual non sequiturs that always

.   .   .   .

bespoke Dole's healthy sense of the surreal in modern politics, even when nobody else could ever quite figure out what he was saying. While the charges were well within the bounds of proper political discussion, concerning not sexual misadventures but lapses within the Clinton White House that the public would do well to consider, such as the business of disappearing and reappearing FBI files, Dole was so uncomfortable that even if he could intellectually make the distinction between public character and private, emotionally he could not and would not. And so, though he stepped up the assault, what it gained in volume and even feigned ferocity it never quite matched in conviction.

In utter frustration, the bomb of Dole rage finally detonated, and the most consummate of contemporary American politicians did what even the least consummate of politicians knows is fatal. Like Jimmy Carter openly bemoaning the public's malaise, Bob Dole openly bemoaned the public's stupidity. The hell with all this raggedy-ass dogshit about drugs, flag-burning, tax cuts and whatever else, none of that mattered, what mattered was that, even as the Democratic Party was awash in everseedier scandals concerning illegal political contributions and shadowy Indonesian power brokers and fund-raisers in Buddhist temples trafficking in laundered money and brazen drug lords dining at the White House, all of which the President's reelection campaign simply dismissed with a breathtaking disdain not dissimilar to Richard Nixon's 1972 reelection campaign, Bob Dole was about to get creamed by the likes of Bill Clinton, a man who ran for attorney general of Arkansas the year that Dole was the Republican nominee for Vice President of the United States. Plainly the very idea was inconceivable to Dole, too absurd and surreal even to a man whom an unapologetically absurd and surreal universe had taught one lesson after another about the cruel vagaries of life going back half a century. And so after first reducing himself to a litany of James Watt bleatings that were beneath him—"He's a liberal! liberal! liberal!" in Georgia, and then, "Defeat liberals and send conservatives to Congress, that's the American way!"—Dole could finally only sputter in disgust to a throng in Florida, "I wonder what the American people are thinking, or if they're thinking at all," moments after it was revealed that he had gone chasing after Ross Perot in Texas, figuratively if not literally, trying to talk Perot out of the race. It was a pitiful display that vaguely recalled George McGovern in 1972 running around futilely begging various Democratic bigshots to be his vice president. Perot characterized Dole's overture as "weird" and momentarily shot up in the polls from 4 percent to 12, before finally splitting the difference at 8.

Given what he must have viewed as the sheer, almost intolerable injustice of losing to a president so transparently unworthy, Dole would only have found it all the more difficult to understand the limits of what even a conservative America could accept. "They're going to have to work out all this Religious Right crap," a retired food caterer told me in Grand Rapids; he had always voted Republican and would vote for Dole, with neither enthusiasm nor expectations. More remarkable were the women I talked to. Young conservative women in their thirties or early forties, Republicans who by almost any definition would be considered pro-life, mothers who were unlikely to ever personally consider having an abortion, who even spoke vaguely of abortion as "death" if not murder, said one after another they would no longer under any circumstances support a candidate for President who was not pro-choice. They had done so in the past, of course, voting for Reagan twice, Bush at least once and sometimes twice, except for the ones who voted for Perot in 1992; almost none had voted in 1992 for Bill Clinton. Almost all would vote for him in 1996. The abortion issue this year, in another instance of how the power of the Religious Right had reached the point of diminishing returns, particularly in the shadow of Gingrich—whom women *despised*—took on a new and vivid pertinence that was much bigger than abortion itself, that had to do with the insult of old men with testicles the size of marbles and prostates the size of bowling balls presuming an insight into the matter of procreation that in fact no man could have, handing down self-righteous dicta to women who had carried life inside them and knew how it felt and what it meant in a way that no man could ever know. In all the ways that the abortion issue had in the past cut so strongly in favor of those who opposed abortion, which is to say those who had voted against abortion above and beyond everything and anything else, this year it was cutting back, women not so much voting for abortion or even for the concept of choice, but for themselves. It was at this moment in the zeitgeist that a perfectly serious solution occurred to me: a national referendum on abortion in which the only Americans allowed to vote were women. But in the meantime they would vote against Bob Dole, who now paid the price for how, in Clintonlike fashion, he had so overhauled and fine-tuned his position on abortion in order to win the Republican nomination in the first place.

Beset as America was by the reality of having to be America, however

. . . .

grandiose the larger contemplations of meaning seemed in comparison to that reality, none of this could contradict how prosaic America had become. The sorrow was that it had become prosaic by necessity: survival of the most prosaic; and you could almost see beyond your windshield America becoming detached from itself, every generation from every other, every race from every other, every town from every other, down to the conjoined American twins of history and memory separating so bloodlessly that, in a weary gesture of such spiritual inertia, it was as though they had never been joined at all. In particular the America that Bill Clinton spoke to, his own generation that was born in nuclear light, felt rebuked on all sides: by disapproving parents, which is to say its past, for whom Bob Dole spoke; by contemptuous children, which is to say its future, for whom no one seemed to speak that hadn't already blown his brains out in a dark Seattle cellar. America might indeed have felt things were being taken care of, but it also felt the gust and hush of what it feared was its own twilight: a huge, preternatural sense that the best of everything was over after all, that having been drained first of all idealism and courage and delirium, it was now drained of the rage that had been the only thing keeping it alive. So in a way this election was not only important, but as the Great Anti-Election at the end of the Twentieth Century, it was perhaps the most important, for the way that, irrefutably and in a roar of silence, the American people were saying in the autumn of 1996 that this election *did not matter to their lives at all.* It had no bearing on them whatsoever, or on whichever America of the mind they or you or anyone else lived in. America had become completely detached from its own voice, not only the words but the mere sound.

As the days dwindled down, it was possible that America just waited to get this election and his Millennium out of the way so as to start something new. It was possible that America had become swallowed up by its own paradox—that having meant to propel itself beyond the dictates of history, having meant from the first to detach history from memory in order to be forever free of the past, as a true country of the imagination, now an America in which schoolchildren did not know which decade the Vietnam War was in or which century the Civil War was in realized that the currency of memory unsupported by the bullion of history was worthless. Now it was possible an America of 250 million different Americas that did not know if they were black or white, slave or slaveowner, righteous or evil, just meant to be finished with Bill Clinton and Bob Dole once and for all and start over, much like Lincoln who, realizing the first

America was beyond salvation, secretly created a second America out of
the Emancipation Proclamation and his speeches at Gettysburg and his
second inauguration. It was possible that the unspoken collective will of
some secret country had resolved, after 250 million secret Antietams,
Shilohs, Chancellorsvilles, Vicksburgs, Bull Runs, Chickamaugas, Cold
Harbors, and Gettysburgs, that the second America was beyond salvation and now a third was to be created, perhaps with the election in the
year 2000 of the man America had really wanted in 1996, and who refused. It was even possible, though a distinct long shot, that a Republican
Party open enough to nominate him, as it had once nominated Lincoln,
could be trusted with such a mission. A year later the country could look
back at Colin Powell's refusal and see precisely the moment when The
Election That Was Supposed To Be instead became The Election The
Country Didn't Want; and so the meaning of America would have to wait
until the country was ready to confront the moment of truth—in a Zone
of Perceived Faith where faith isn't now or never—as to whether it still
had the faith to make Joe Christmas President of the United States. And
while one would not want to sink into messianic illusions about Powell,
or suspend reservations about putting a career military man in the chair
of commander-in-chief (though it didn't work out so badly with Washington or Eisenhower, who knew enough about the military to be unim-
pressed by it), there could be no overstating the sheer transformative
symbolism of a black man's election, as much as the hardheaded might
want to argue such symbolism was just liberal goo. If and when such a
thing came to pass there could be no pretending that a third America,
hopefully and presumably still bonded to the first two by the Declaration
of Independence and the Constitution, was not at hand.

You drive down I-55 from Chicago and turn left at St. Louis, and drive
another ten minutes outside St. Louis and, as dusk falls, find the grave of
Cahokia. Cahokia is the great lost America: not utopia, not Atlantis, not a
myth, not an alternative or parallel America, but as much America the
Real in the Thirteenth Century as the America the Real of the Twentieth.
The Americans of Cahokia, whom scientists now call Mississippians for
where the Mississippi, Illinois, and Missouri rivers met, built the greatest
city of its time, a city greater than London or Paris, greater than the cities
of the Mayans who were already on the wane, the greatest of all American
cities until the New York City of the Nineteenth Century, stretching over
seventy miles and populated by twenty thousand Americans who built at
Cahokia's center a pyramid fifty feet high. Now this pyramid lies beneath

the mounds of earth that roll southwest to the Ozarks. But if you are somewhere on the road just between a momentary stability and the craziness that's been waiting for you around the bend, you might almost see at dusk 20,000 American ghosts rise from the grave of this America that was secret from the rest of the world, secret from history, the last America that presumed it might cut off history from memory once and for all, before it died. Its death remains unfixed by science. There are no earthly shows of trauma by cataclysm, either natural or manmade, no gashes of devastating war, there is no sign of rot from some sweeping plague. There are only the geological and archeological hints of social suicide, of an America that slipped away into a great catatonia of the soul, cavalierly ravishing the land and water around it until the land and water could offer nothing in return, an America indulging itself into a fatal national lethargy until, as the desperation of the situation suddenly became clear, it was too late, when those who had less were repressed by those who had more, when resentment just answered resentment and a meeker nihilism was answered by a nihilism more rapacious. And when you pull up to the curb of Cahokia and gaze across the grave of the secret country you may find yourself, not unlike a ghost, suddenly set free of history and memory after all, floating to some place that knows neither nation nor millennium— which is all we ever really wanted of America to begin with.

But driving homeward, wherever home happens to be at the moment, that safe space you have commandeered between stability and craziness, between the history that made you and the memory that names you, cracks apart. On those occasions when you remember how lost you are, the half-moment that it surprises you meets the half-moment you knew it was there all the time, which threatens to leave you scrambling toward whatever dark passion still makes you feel like an American. By now you've spent days or weeks or months draping your life on one prosaic function after another in an interminable series of prosaic functions that are accepted, performed, accounted for, and cashed in exchange for the luxury of telling yourself that you're functioning, since the only alternative is the breakdown that your pride and ego and instinct for survival won't allow you to have but that your heart has been begging for. And then finally there's just one function, without significance or metaphor, that's more than you can hang your life on; and when your life sags, you peer over it and see the gaping black beyond and it catches your breath. Then you would like to offer, as an answer to that void, an approximation in yourself of something just as black, but unless you're Charles Manson or Jeffrey Dahmer or Jesse Helms such a feeling is too far beneath you to be touched, let alone articulated. On the car stereo is not Sinatra or Springsteen but another Jersey punk, except that whereas Sinatra and even Springsteen always sang so as to never be called punks again, Patti Smith always sang so as to ennoble the title, presenting herself as the maternal nexus between Dylan who sang for young America's ideals and Cobain who sang for young America's despair. Patti sings over and over of death and though in your head you know she sings of resurrection too, as history slips behind you and memory rushes toward you, just outside your windshield the dying is all you can hear. You finally turn the tape player off, the radio on, and almost as a joke the radio immediately plays a Kurt Cobain song; and the pathetic and monstrous passion that left him still feeling alive before it felt too bad to be alive is beyond any ideology that could either drain his desire of rage or his violence of need.

This is an American pain translated into a passion that's beyond excuses, let alone redemption. It is a passion that has no faith, hard as you try for it; it is a passion that finally only serves the function of keeping you alive because you know that without it you would just blow your head off. It's possible that you've never seen yourself as faithless, that the recurring image of a gun in all your American songs is just a whimsical coincidence. It's possible that you would give just as much—everything—for your ideals as you do for your despair, that your wrathful and lovely country, blistered by loss as it is, was always intended as the testament of some affirmation you have never really believed you deserve, your own ideals muttered from the dreamy aquahaze of lithium and heroin:

> I'm so happy because today
> I've found my friends,
> they're in my head.
> I'm so ugly but that's OK, so are you,
> we've broken our mirrors.
> Sunday morning is everyday for all I care,
> I'm not scared.
> Light my candles in a daze,
> because I've found God

at which point the song comes crashing down on you, having been launched from under the surface of its own melody and ripping skyward faster than the speed and ascent of its own sound; the half-moment that it

．　．　．　．　．　．　．　．　．　．

charges you with the bellow of its refusal to succumb to either delusion or pain or anything else meets the half-moment that it terrorizes you with its passion. When you were younger and America was vast before you, the test of your country's meaning was whether it had the power to frighten and change you, driving alone on I-55 at night and heading back one last time to Chicago. And the test of your country's meaning was whether, as time passed, the fear turned to a terrible exhilaration, in part because you learned to live with the fear and in part because you were left with no choice but to be liberated by it since there was no becoming liberated from it. Then one night in history the nature of fear changed, maybe it was the night the Wall came down and there was nothing on the other side to be afraid of anymore except for some horror too personal to tear down as easily as a wall; somewhere in the dark, somewhere in that void beyond the sag of your life from a line of failed functions, somebody buried your secret country in the mud, and the darkness that came roaring over the horizon was the shadow of the Secret Millennium and though it should have been everyone's shadow, it was somehow only yours. Before the edge of the shadow touches us, the meaning of America has become the way we're so willing to challenge and offend every value but the one we blindly hold as true. At the intersection of assault and nurturing, you will either turn the music up, or off. Forgetting the pain again that you never wanted to remember in the first place, returning to your life of functions, you may opt for off. But sooner or later there will be no more forgetting, the re-membering will be irrevocable, and then off is just another function. Up is a direction.

. . . .

CHARLES BAXTER is the author of *First Light, Shadow Play, Harmony of the World, Through the Safety Net, A Relative Stranger, Believers,* and a first collection of nonfiction, *Burning Down the House.* He was recently honored with an Academy Award in Literature from the American Academy of Arts and Letters.

RICHARD BAUSCH is the author of many books of fiction. *The Selected Stories of Richard Bausch* was published by the Modern Library. His most recent novel is *In the Night Season.* He is Heritage Professor of Writing at George Mason University.

KAREN BRENNAN is the author of an AWP award book of stories, *Wild Desire,* published by the University of Massachusetts Press.

BERNARD COOPER is the author of *Maps to Anywhere* and most recently a collection of memoirs, *Truth Serum.* He is the recipient of the 1991 PEN/USA Ernest Hemingway Award and a 1995 O. Henry Prize. He lives in Los Angeles.

LYDIA DAVIS is the author of several books of short fiction, most recently *Almost No Memory,* published by Farrar, Straus & Giroux. She is also the author of a novel, *The End of the Story.* She is currently translating Proust's *Swann's Way* for Penguin Books.

STEVE ERICKSON lives in Los Angeles. He is the author of six novels, most recently *The Sea Came In at Midnight,* to be published by Bard in spring 1999, and a book about the 1996 Presidential election, *American Nomad.*

ALVIN GREENBERG is a poet, fiction writer, and essayist. His most recent book of short fiction is *How the Dead Live.* He teaches literature and creative writing at Macalester College.

PATRICIA HAMPL has written extensively on memoir and is the author of three nonfiction books, *A Romantic Education, Spillville,* and *Virgin Time.* She teaches at the University of Minnesota.

MARGOT LIVESEY is the author of a book of stories and two novels, most recently *Criminals.* She was born in Scotland and currently lives in Cambridge.

JAMES A. MCPHERSON teaches in the University of Iowa MFA program. He is the author of two books of stories, *Hue and Cry* and *Elbow Room,* and a memoir, *Crabcakes.* He has been awarded a MacArthur Fellowship and the Pulitzer Prize.

VICTORIA MORROW is currently a student in the MFA program at the University of Michigan. She has had stories published in *ACM, Fish Stories,* and *Hidden River.*

MICHAEL RYAN is the author of three books of poetry, most recently *God Hunger,* and a memoir, *Secret Life.* He has won the Yale Series of Younger Poets Award, NEA and Guggenheim Fellowships, a Whiting Writers Award, and the Lenore Marshall/*Nation* Award. He teaches at the MFA Writing Programs at Warren Wilson College and at the University of California at Irvine.

SYLVIA WATANABE teaches at Oberlin College. She was born in Hawaii on the island of Maui. She is the recipient of a Japanese American Citizens League National Literary Award and a fellowship from the National Endowment for the Arts and was a 1991 O. Henry award winner. She is the author of *Talking to the Dead and Other Stories* published by Doubleday.

This series was designed by Will Powers. It is set in Sabon and Formata type by Stanton Publication Services, Inc. and manufactured by Bang Printing on acid-free paper.